T0165728

WARNING:

DRIVER EDUCATION CAN KILL YOUR TEENAGER

PATRICK BARRETT

WARNING:

DRIVER EDUCATION CAN KILL YOUR TEENAGER

Published by Advantage, Charleston, South Carolina.
Member of Advantage Media Group.

ADVANTAGE is a registered trademark and the Advantage colophon is a trademark of Advantage Media Group, Inc.

Printed in the United States of America.

ISBN: 978-159932-401-2
LCCN: 2013940815

This publication is designed to provide accurate and authoritative information in regard to the subject matter covered. It is sold with the understanding that the publisher is not engaged in rendering legal, accounting, or other professional services. If legal advice or other expert assistance is required, the services of a competent professional person should be sought.

Advantage Media Group is proud to be a part of the Tree Neutral® program. Tree Neutral offsets the number of trees consumed in the production and printing of this book by taking proactive steps such as planting trees in direct proportion to the number of trees used to print books. To learn more about Tree Neutral, please visit **www.treeneutral.com**. To learn more about Advantage's commitment to being a responsible steward of the environment, please visit **www.advantagefamily.com/green**

Advantage Media Group is a publisher of business, self-improvement, and professional development books and online learning. We help entrepreneurs, business leaders, and professionals share their Stories, Passion, and Knowledge to help others Learn & Grow™. Do you have a manuscript or book idea that you would like us to consider for publishing? Please visit **advantagefamily.com** or call **1.866.775.1696.**

Driver Ed in a Box® is a registered trademark of Patrick Barrett.

TABLE OF
CONTENTS

WHO I AM AND WHY YOU SHOULD LISTEN TO ME

Kristen got ready for school that morning as she got ready every morning. She drank her orange juice, and ate her cereal. Then she packed her essentials—cell phone and book bag—and slipped out the side door to her car. She picked up her friend Ashley, bound for a typical day of high school, but about a mile from their destination, tragedy struck.

We don't know if the two were chatting as best friends do, or if Kristen was blinded by the early morning sun shooting through the trees. All we know for sure is that she pulled out from a side street onto the main road in front of a dump truck. Neither driver had time to react, and two promising lives were lost. It's a tragedy that ended the lives of two young girls and tore apart the lives of many more, yet it was completely preventable.

Kristen got an A in her driver education class and passed the state road test with flying colors. She was a cheerleader, a good student, and by all accounts, a responsible young girl who was loved and trusted by her parents. How could this happen? After all, Kristen had attended the driving school in town and met all the requirements the state mandated for her to get her driver license. As far as she, her family, the state, and her driving school instructor were concerned, Kristen was a safe and knowledgeable driver. I've heard too many stories like Kristen and Ashley's. This type of event, the unnecessary death of two teenagers, occurs thousands of times every year in the United States. If all of these lives had been lost to an infection or a disease, the Center for Disease Control (CDC) would alert the nation every day about the dangers of this disease.

Why is this happening? Why has driver education failed to make new drivers safer drivers?

Blood money. That's exactly what almost all driver education in the United States is: blood money.

Millions of new drivers (and even some experienced drivers) are required to pay hundreds of dollars for courses that ensure that they know just enough to be dangerous to themselves and others.

The businesses that create or produce courses, course materials, and instructor courses, the driving schools that sell these courses, and their advocates are only concerned about making money, having job security, and forcing people to take their courses as a prerequisite for obtaining a driver license. And where it's not a prerequisite, teenager drivers must wait an additional six months to two years to get their license if they did not complete such a course. Driver education, in some form, is required for early licensing in 37 states in the United States. Vendors and advocates of driver education courses have spent huge amounts of money to guarantee that they have a customer base that is essentially a captive audience.

They devote little, if any, attention to discovering what produces safe drivers. Consequently, laws requiring driver education (and traffic ticket dismissal courses, aka traffic schools) set minimal standards that simply create the illusion that these mandated programs make drivers safer.

If you are the parent of a teenager who drives or is about to drive, you need to understand that if you meet the state's minimum requirements to get your teen her driver's license so she can drive on her own, you are playing Russian roulette with her life—and the lives of others.

Here are the facts:

- The Center for Disease Control and Prevention reported in 2010 that the cost of medical care and productivity losses associated with motor vehicle crash injuries was over $99 billion, or nearly $500, for each licensed driver in the United States. In addition, every 10 seconds, an American is treated in an emergency department for crash-related injuries, based on data from 2005.

- In 2011, 32,367 people died in motor vehicle traffic crashes in the United States

- In 2011, an estimated 2.22 million people were injured in motor vehicle traffic crashes

Source: NCSA Research Note: "2011 Motor Vehicle Crashes: Overview"

(DOT-HS-811-701)

U.S. DOT TRAFFIC SAFETY FACTS

2010 National Statistics
Police-Reported Motor Vehicle Traffic Crashes

Fatal 30,196

Injury 1,542,000

Property Damage Only 3,847,000

Total 5,419,000

If you want to do something about reducing the number of crashes that involve teenagers and cost us dearly in terms of dollars and so much more in terms of the families' unending heartache, then pay attention and read on. Here's your chance to clearly grasp why we have this problem and how you can become part of the solution that can eliminate more than half of these crashes.

Yes, we can train a beginner to become a safe driver. Yes, we can eliminate crashes by 50 percent. But it cannot be done with the standards and laws that now require beginners to take traditional driver education.

I know we can reduce driving accidents because I've done it on a small scale. I have had clients in the telecommunications business and in the utility business who contracted with me to reduce their collision rates. Their technicians and service people were located in almost every major city in the United States. I designed and implemented a driver safety training program that resulted in the reduction of their collision rates by 60 percent to 78 percent. Since they kept accurate records and were self-insured, we were able to accurately identify their collision rates. Although I was paid a nominal fee for the training, I only earned my bonus if I reduced their collision rate by at least 50 percent. This was a win-win for everyone involved.

I've made it my life's mission is to reduce automobile collisions in the United States by 50 percent. I set that goal decades ago and although I have developed training systems that can accomplish the task, I can't do it alone. I need your help.

I'm Patrick Barrett.

I am the nation's leading driver education and training expert, having trained more than 75,000 collision-free drivers. A 2006 study by the Texas Department of Public Safety Teen Driver Records showed that 16-year-olds who received graduation certificates after using my driver education methodology had a **collision rate six times lower** than the collision rate of all 16-year-old drivers in Texas.

Even though I'm a certified teacher with over 35 years of experience in driver education and even though at one time I owned the largest driving school in Texas, I can't reach my goal alone. I need the support of many people who understand and appreciate how I can protect their children's lives by making their children safer drivers.

What makes my plan worth your time and attention is that my experience is different. I've probably experimented more than anyone else in our field, not with just the business side of driver education but also with the teaching side of it to find out what really works, what's really necessary to make someone a safer driver. It isn't enough just to help someone learn to move, to start, stop, turn, and park a vehicle, or to talk about what they should be doing.

What matters to me are results. What do we really have to do to teach a beginner, or for that matter, even an experienced driver? What must we do to help that person become a collision-free driver? What are the techniques that are absent from today's driver education? What are the processes for teaching those techniques?

That's what I've committed to study and learn and perfect over these last several decades. The results my clients in the utilities and telecommunications businesses have experienced (a reduction of over 50 percent in their collision rates) and the results experienced by beginner drivers who use my system (a collision rate that is over six times lower than other programs and courses) are proof that we can reduce the crashes young people experience in this country by 50 percent.

I learned from experts who had actually gone decades without having collisions in their fleet. When I was president of the North American Professional Driver Education Association, I sought out the leading trainers of fleets (government and private industry) and elite driver-training business owners. I either took specific training from them or developed mastermind groups that met several times a year for years. With this process I discovered what they had in common and how I could implement their successful techniques in a short, easy, simple, and clear fashion. I had to be efficient because, with some of my clients, I was only permitted a limited amount of time to do my job. I had to improve the performance my clients' driving and make sure the training would stick so they would not be involved in a collision once I left. If I didn't produce results, I didn't get paid.

After successful results working with those clients, I adapted a program to apply these unique techniques to teaching beginners. It was the first program of its kind. People in driver education and traffic safety talk about wanting safe drivers, but the fact is they don't understand the teaching process itself, never mind how to create safer drivers.

Yet it is the process that's important, and that's what I focus on—in addition to the techniques that I have learned in my many years in the business. And that's what I will teach you in this book. You can access the resources you need to ensure that your son or daughter becomes a safe driver at **www.FREEdriverEdTexas.com**. The real reason you should listen to me is because you don't want to bury your child or see him as an invalid, bound to a wheelchair, devoid of his mental faculties, and unable to take care of his personal needs. No one wants that for their child, especially if it was avoidable.

I'm one of eight kids. I grew up in a very strict Catholic family. My parents were devout Catholics. My father was a daily communicant and an honest businessman. Mom and Dad sacrificed time, money, and worldly possessions to send all eight of us to Catholic schools. They believed in and followed the teachings of the church. Mom and Dad did their best to make sure all of us did the same.

Mom and Dad had a strong work ethic (growing up in the Great Depression probably contributed to that) and they passed that along to each of us.

There's a little story that you'll be able to read later in this book about a day at Dad's shop. It was truly a thrill for my older brother and I to get up on Saturday mornings, hop in Dad's truck (Jay usually got the window seat), and head off to work in the shop—or at least that's what we called it. It was a little heating and air-conditioning business in downtown Alton, Illinois. The family business was started in 1896 by my great-grandfather as a sheet metal company. Over the years, my dad expanded the business to include heating and air-conditioning, and six of my brothers and sisters are still involved in that business today. It looks like there's another generation coming along that may carry on the proud family tradition. What did I learn as a kid on those Saturdays at the shop while other kids were playing at the park? I learned the value of a good work ethic: to always do my best on any job I had. Unfortunately, I didn't always take that advice. Sometimes I did just enough to get by. When I got caught (and I usually did), I ended up paying the price. I'd have to redo the task, this time under the watchful eye of the angry boss (Mom or Dad) and I didn't like that one bit.

It seemed as though I was always working, as though Jay and I spent every Saturday and holiday in the shop. We also had newspaper routes that stayed in our family for 13 years. Throwing newspapers, collecting the money on Saturdays—that was a great experience.

I have to admit when my younger sister Cathy told the paper route manager that we would deliver the morning *St. Louis Dispatch*, I wasn't thrilled because I was in high school at the time and I had to get up at 4:30 a.m. We lived in Alton, Illinois, about twenty miles north of St. Louis, and thus very few people took the St. Louis paper, so I had to walk three times the territory for about half the pay, not a great arrangement. But my mom said a promise was a promise, so we did the job.

We started in January. Oh, it was cold, so cold we had to put a light bulb attached to an extension cord from the house just to keep the oil from freezing in the trucks! Single digit temperatures and biting winds were common. I fell asleep a couple of times in class at the high school simply because I was exhausted. The teacher, a nun, kindly let me doze off, but occasionally my classmates took all my books and distributed them to desks around the room so when I woke up I had to go hunt for my books. Ah, the joys of being a teenager!

I mowed lawns. I worked as a life guard at the YMCA, the YWCA, and the local college. We'd do odd jobs for people who wanted help with organizing or cleaning out their homes. But the summertime was always reserved for the shop. As I got closer to going off to college, I became less enamored with working there. The day after high-school graduation, I started working there full time. It was not fun. I had to do maintenance on an air conditioning unit despite unsteady footing on the roof. I had to apply glue to the bottom of the air conditioning unit and then slide two-inch-thick yellow fiberglass-type insulation wedges under the unit. I ended up lying on the hot roof, trying to get the insulation material in the right spot. The insulation scraped against my arms and face. Ignoring my pain, I pressed the insulation against the bottom of the unit to make sure it stuck in place. My face and arms itched for a week after that, and I swore that if I could ever find another job—any kind of job—I would quit working at the shop. I had to find two other jobs to earn enough to allow me to go to college in the fall—and believe me, I found them.

I ended up as a baseball umpire at night for the city's recreation department, and during the day I worked as a timekeeper on a construction site. A couple of years later, I coached a local swim team in the summer. I did that for three summers. I loved coaching. The kids were great and the parents were fantastic. At the end of that third summer, just as I was going into the first fall of my teaching career, I realized that as much as I loved coaching swimming, this was not going to be my life's work. I wasn't going to be a swim coach. My destiny would be elsewhere.

If you had told me I would devote most of my life to helping people become safer drivers, I would have thought you were crazy.

The fact is that when I got into the driver education business, I really didn't plan to stay in it very long. I only planned to work for a summer. The two courses I needed to complete my master's degree (in religious education) from St. Louis University weren't available

19

until the fall. I was going to work in driver education for the summer and then go back to school in the fall.

But it didn't work out that way. Soon, I'm teaching six or seven days a week for a driving school. By winter I'm training their instructors. Six months after that, I move from being an assistant manager at the St. Louis branch to opening and managing a new location for the company in Kansas City. A few months later, I'm transferred to Houston to operate that office.

Unfortunately, the owner of the company was a crook (he's now a convicted felon). He was convicted of insurance fraud, making and collecting on false claims from crashes that may or may not have happened.

I knew the company was involved in a lot of crashes. All the managers talked about them. The discussion was always, "How many did you have and how bad were they?" See, because everyone had accidents, I assumed that simply came with the business. All you could hope for was to minimize your losses.

When I started my own driving school in 1978, here in Houston, I was afraid that too many crashes would end my fledgling business. I trained my instructors thoroughly. In fact, I trained them so well that other schools sought out people that I had trained and fired. I later found out that my rejects were their best instructors.

Like many start-up owners, I was not earning much of a living. A friend of mine had a saying on a plaque on his desk: "Why work for someone else for forty hours, when you can work for yourself for eighty hours at half the pay?" I would have been glad to get at least half the pay during those first few years! (I realize this is not a very good business model to follow.) I would have made more money if I had been working at McDonald's flipping hamburgers. I was about to throw in the towel after the second year.

Occasionally, I'd receive newsletters from an organization called the North American Professional Driver Education Association. I became curious and thought I'd take a look before I threw in the towel.

In Toronto, Heinz Naumann, from the Young Drivers of Canada, hosted an event. It was the North American Professional Driver Education Association's annual convention. In talking to some of the other business owners, I asked about accidents. "How do you fellows handle accidents?" They said, "We don't have them." I said, "What do you mean you don't have them?" They said, "You take this special training from the association and you don't have to worry about having accidents anymore."

I found that hard to believe. I thought these guys were blowing smoke. I just couldn't believe it. I saw Heinz's operation. It was very impressive and I realized that they were doing things we were not, such as making a decent profit. So I thought I'd go back to Houston and renew my efforts.

A few weeks later, I scheduled in-vehicle training in Chicago to see if they could teach me something I didn't already know. Holy cow! What a surprise! It was an eye opener for me. I couldn't believe how much I didn't know about teaching people how to stay out of collisions.

Immediately after I'd taken that forty-hour-plus in-vehicle training, I came back to Houston and trained all my instructors so thoroughly that in the 11 years after that, we never made an insurance claim. This was remarkable, considering that at one time I had over 50 instructors teaching in-vehicle driving.

Warren Rumsfield, founder of the North American Professional Driver Education Association, became my mentor and very good friend. He recognized the need to put in writing a lot of our concepts regarding training techniques.

We collaborated on numerous books and articles about how to teach people to drive safely. We created *Safe Driving Habits*, a textbook for beginners. This student text was used by the better driving schools across the country. We also created *Building Safe Driving Habits*, a guide to teaching driving techniques. We created other published materials and conducted conferences and seminars across the country and at the Chicago office. After Warren's death in 1986, I continued to conduct conferences and seminars, and I have written and created additional books, pamphlets, articles, and customized programs on driver education.

By 1988 I had become dissatisfied with the driving school business because I felt the public deserved so much more than what the state and the industry required. I sold all ten of my schools. At that time, I had the largest driving school in Texas. We were serving over 40,000 clients a year (including beginning teen and adult students, plus experienced drivers taking a corporate or ticket dismissal course), but we were not getting the results that I thought were possible.

Then I chose to go into fleet work. I customized and implemented safe driver programs for corporate clients. I would spend a day or two with the employees who drove company vehicles. I would review the company's accident reports. Then I would develop a program that included a brief classroom orientation (30 to 40 minutes) followed by an intense in-vehicle, on-the-street training session in real-world traffic (3 to 3½ hours) in groups of up to five participants.

The client would only let employees train for a few hours. With that limitation in mind, I had to cut out all the fluff and only work on the core items that would produce the desired result: a minimum of a 50 percent reduction of collisions. I guaranteed the company that I would reduce its collision rate by 50 percent after three years or it wouldn't have to pay me, which was leverage for the client and an incentive for me.

I have never failed to reduce collision rates by over 50 percent. Because my clients self-insure, they have real numbers that reflect the millions (or tens of millions) of dollars I save them each year. A company that self-insures pays for its losses out of its pocket. Some clients paid losses up to two million dollars; some paid losses up to two hundred million. Their insurance company would not get involved until the loss exceeded the amount that had been self-insured.

My years of training fleet drivers demanded that I train folks in almost every major city in the United States, which gave me a wealth of experience unique to my field. Remember, this is real-world training in traffic, where it counts. Eventually, I was able to grow that business enough to where I had others I could train in my system and allow them to train others in my system.

Of course, there's a difference between professional drivers— adults who have been driving for 10, 15, or 20 years—and teenagers. Teenagers do not have years of experience to draw from and their prefrontal cortex (the part of the brain that is needed for judgment) is not yet fully developed.

But there are also a number of similarities among the two groups. The same fundamentals that have to be taught (or retaught) to an experienced driver are the very fundamentals that beginners have to learn. For the most part, beginners are not being trained in these fundamentals and that's why motor vehicle crashes kill more teenagers than anyone else.

So when I re-entered the teenage driver education market in 1997, I took all the things that I had learned from working with the fleets and incorporated them into the training of beginner drivers.

Also I created special tools to help parents guide their teenagers through that process. These unique tools and training devices (such as the extensive use of commentary, the forward and reverse pivot points, the focus on eye movement, the audio and video series that guide the parent and the student through the in-vehicle training, the in-vehicle checklists, and the dual instructor mirrors) have been well received by both parents and teens.

Driver Ed in a Box® is a family business. My wife, Frances, and I started it and our sons, John and Warren, are involved in it too. Today, Frances doesn't work much at all (the result of "chemo brain" from her cancer treatments). John handles the operations end of the business, and Warren, because he hasn't sold his first screenplay yet, helps us with the filming and the editing of the audios and videos we produce.

Like my dad's family business, ours is designed to help us make a decent living and provide a good service for our clients. The motto of my high school, Marquette High School in Alton, Illinois, is *Serviam* (I serve.) That commitment of service has been an important part of my life.

I have become a reluctant leader in this field. I never intended to be a leader in this or any other field. My goal was to be a team member—a significant contributor to the team—in sports, at work, or in the family.

When my freshman high-school coach told me I was going to play quarterback instead of fullback, I accepted the challenge and learned how to play that position. When Warren Rumsfield, Bonnie Kittelson, and Chuck Keessee asked me to become the president of the North American Professional Driver Education Association, I stepped up to the plate and developed the skills I needed to do that job.

I could have said no, but I didn't, and I served in that position for eight years.

I've had to pay close attention to legislative activity, speak to legislatures, and testify at hearings in the legislature every other year in Texas since 1999 to ensure that the laws allowing parents to teach are not eliminated or diminished. In every session, a bill has been presented that is designed to take away or diminish the ability of parents to teach their children how to drive without their having to attend a public or private driving school. This is not an issue of public safety. It's an issue of market share. The driving schools and public schools do not want to face a situation where the public is not required to take a course from them because they are not accustomed to selling their course on its own merits or creating value for their customers.

The price of freedom is eternal vigilance.

CHAPTER
TWO

AN UNEXPECTED JOURNEY: HOW I GOT HERE

My company, Driver Ed in a Box, was borne out of personal frustration regarding Texas state driver education policies and the expectation of parents. In 1997 I was hot and heavy in the fleet business. I was working from dawn to dusk, it seemed, when I was traveling, and that's when the law actually came into effect in Texas. Actually, the law changed in 1995, but the Texas Department of Public Safety (DPS) dragged its feet for two years and refused to actually implement the law. It's not the only time it has done that.

For instance, in 2009 I helped author legislation (House Bill 339) in Texas that requires the DPS to track the collision rates of graduates of driver education courses, based on where they took their course, and to publish those collision rates. That is, each individual driving school, public or private, and each individual, state-approved, at-home course provider would have their students' collision rates tracked and published by the DPS. As of this writing, the DPS has failed to accurately track and publish this data.

The purpose of that section of Texas House Bill 339 was to provide information that would help the public make an informed choice of driver education schools or programs and legislators and regulators identify best practices. Parents looking at their options for driver education could base their selection of a school or course on the collision rates of school or course graduates. This would be akin to knowing the success rate of a particular doctor or hospital when you are making a decision about surgery. Imagine how valuable that information could be.

In 1997, the year the law changed in Texas and parents could now teach driver education to their teenagers without having to use the service of a public or private driving school, I had a sixteen-year-old who wanted to get his driver's license. I sure wasn't going to send him to driving school. I knew what was going on in most of these schools and I didn't want him going through that. Fortunately, the law became effective in May of that year.

We had homeschooled one of our kids, Michael, for a couple of years, and we discovered in that process that there were some very, very diligent parents who made an earnest effort to make sure that their children got a good education. There wasn't much in driver education for homeschoolers, although the homeschool community had been the leading force in making sure that the law was passed in the state of Texas, especially the Texas Home School Coalition.

I had talked to some of my friends who were still in the driving school business to see if they were going to provide any parent-taught courses, and they just said no. They thought it was a waste of time. Since the state was going to provide free courses, they saw no potential profit in competing with that. The DPS charged a $20 registration fee and then sent the curriculum guidelines to the parents. The DPS used that $20 to pay for a unique certificate that they purchased from the Texas Education Agency and maintained on file to verify that parents and students were eligible to use a parent-taught approved course.

There certainly wasn't anyone more qualified than me to teach my son to drive. So I paid my $20 registration fee to the state, which mailed me a packet of material. The packet was about two inches thick. I read it all. It took me a couple of hours to get through it even though I was quite familiar with the content. I told Frances, "Honey, it's a good thing I already know what I'm supposed to do because nobody can figure it out from this thing."

Essentially, what the DPS did was copy the Texas Education Agency's materials for driver-education teachers and send it out to parents. A lot of parents, after receiving their packet from the state, simply threw up their hands and enrolled their teen in the nearest driving school. I suspect that was the result the DPS wanted because it never supported parent-taught driver education.

The fact is I wouldn't have been a supporter of parent-taught driver education 20 years ago. If that idea had come in the early nineties, I would have thought "Uh-oh, parents are the worst ones to be teaching them because their habits are so poor. (I know how poor their habits are because I worked with fleets, and most drivers have a lot of poor habits. Even people who were conscientiously trying to be good drivers would backslide into dangerous habits.) Plus, parents are not trained in how to communicate with their teen in this particular arena, and their confusion about how to teach could lead to a crash. Maybe they'll be able to help their son or daughter move the car but, at best, most of these teens will know just enough to be dangerous. I think they should be going to schools."

That's what I would have thought 20 years ago.

Because of my experience with homeschooling, I believed there might be some people who were conscientious enough to do a good job. But they needed the right tools. I thought that if we created the materials for them and showed them what to do and how to do it, they could do as well, if not better, than most driver-education teachers. They wouldn't be marking time, which is when the instructor simply rides around, checking his watch to make sure he and his student get back in time. It's like people in an office who kill time by chatting with coworkers or hanging out at the water cooler; like employees who get off at 5 p.m. but at three o'clock have already quit mentally and are just going through the motions to fill time before they leave. Driver-education teachers even have a phrase for this: "Let's go drive the student."—not "let's go instruct." Their objective is usually to put in their time and get paid.

Instead of doing only the minimum required to get a license, parents could take their time and continue to train and practice until their teen learned to be safe and mastered certain skills. If we showed parents how to teach our system, they could actually produce safer drivers than those coming out of the schools.

I wondered if there was a market for what we had to offer. Would parents be willing to invest in our product to protect their sons and daughters? I didn't know if this would be a success or a bomb. Nevertheless, I took the leap.

In June 1997 I placed an ad in the yellow pages. The phone book didn't come out until the fall. That's when we started to get some business.

I was working on the east coast when the phone books were delivered. I returned after a particularly grueling trip: flight delays, bad food, and sleep deprivation. I was dragging my weary tail and travel bag up the sidewalk, looking forward to a weekend of rest and recovery. But that was not going to happen.

Upon my return, Frances was standing at the door waving a check in her hand, saying, "We got an order! We got an order!" I asked, "Okay. honey, is there anything that we haven't created yet?" She said, "Yeah, you haven't done the audio series."

So that's what I did that weekend. I took a table, put my recorder on it, sat on the edge of my bed, and recorded the six-audio-tape series, which is still the basis of the audio series that we have today. In 1997 it was on cassettes. I actually had made six two-sided cassettes, or about 300 minutes of audio. I had already gone over in my mind what parents would need to hear. I sketched out an outline and knocked it out. It wasn't as if I hadn't done it before. I'd trained hundreds of teachers and I knew exactly what they needed to go through and what adjustments they'd have to make in order to do this job effectively.

I created that audio series in one weekend. I had a duplicating machine so I'd duplicate the cassettes as we needed them. Frances made the labels. So we'd slap those on, put them in an audio cassette case with a nice cover, and they were good to go. That first order went out Monday morning. There was not much business at first. In fact, in the first three years we didn't make much money at all. I told Frances, "Honey, we're losing less money every month." She was okay with that because we weren't losing much and after four months we started breaking even. Eventually, we started making a little money.

After the fourth year, I was making more money from Driver Ed in the Box than I was from my fleet work simply because we were getting a lot of word-of-mouth recommendations. We were happy with that. Today, much of our business comes from people who refer their friends or relatives to us. We greatly appreciate the referrals.

Every legislative year, I would go back to the legislature. Driving schools and public schools were trying to knock out parent-taught driver education and the Texas DPS wasn't any help either. I'd attended a traffic safety conference and listened to driver education instructors, administrators, and regulators talk. They ranted against parent-taught driver education even though it was the law of the land. The Texas DPS didn't make it easy for parents to choose this option. On several occasions, they harassed the parents when they were at the driver license office trying to get through the process. There's a little less of that today, but I believe there are still elements in the Texas DPS that oppose parent-taught driver education.

During hearings in the legislature, we'd hear anecdotes, not facts, presented as reasons for doing away with parent-taught driver education. What were the facts? No one appeared to have any real data, so I thought we needed to find out how effective parent-taught driver education was. At the very least, I was curious as to how our graduates' driving records compared to other courses and methods of delivery.

For two years in a row, I obtained the driving records of a thousand of our graduates. I wanted to see how their collision rate compared to the overall collision rates of comparably aged teens. I had used this same formula before when I worked with the fleets. Scientific or not, it gave us an indication of whether or not something was working. The fleets I had as clients knew what they were paying out in their cost of collisions. They knew how many collisions they had. They kept records because they were self-insured.

I simply applied the same formula to assessing the effectiveness of Driver Ed in a Box. I got the collision records from the DPS for everybody in the state, the age, number of collisions, and number of licensed drivers. It's easy to calculate the collision rate with that data.

The collision rate for all the 16-year-olds in the state of Texas was 11.4 percent. Our Driver Ed in a Box graduates had a collision rate of less than 2 percent. I thought that was just amazing.

In 2009 I provided the language for a bill (HB 339 of the 81st Legislature) to require the Texas DPS to annually track and publish the collision-rate data of graduates of driver-education courses, based on the individual school and course provider. The purpose was to give the public the opportunity to make an informed choice about driver education and, over time, to provide data to identify the best practices in driver education. As of this writing (2013), the Texas DPS has still not accurately collected and published the data.

It may seem counterintuitive, but driver education will never be effective in reducing collisions as long as it is conducted in public schools or as long as it is regulated by standards set by state education agencies and motor vehicle departments.

Learning to drive safely is an important skill. It is a vital skill, but it stands no chance of being taught in a public school because an effective course requires one-on-one instruction (around 70 to 200 hours of training and supervised practice). We don't have the data for exactly how many hours, simply because learning these skills varies from one person to another. It depends on the person, the time, and resources that person and instructor devote to the skill, and other factors such the environment (weather, time of day, distance from a practice area, etc.).

DISCOVERING THE SECRET SAUCE

My mentor, Warren Rumsfield, who began the North American Professional Driver Education Association in 1956, was a public school teacher with the Chicago public schools. To earn extra money, he started a driving school with one of his buddies in the summer. One step led to another and the next thing he knew, he had 75 cars in the driving school. His driving school income dwarfed his public-school salary.

One big problem his driving school faced was the number of accidents his fleet experienced. He was so scared about losing his auto insurance he would devote three days of instructor training to what instructors should do if involved in an accident. It wasn't whether or not it was going to happen. It was what to do when it did happen because accidents were going to happen. You couldn't avoid them.

During those three days of intense training, the instructors were taught to do whatever they could do to make sure his company was not liable for the crash: check the other driver's car to see if it had a broken headlight; see if the other driver had a windshield that was dirty and impaired the driver's view; see if any alcohol could be smelled on the other driver's breath; get the names and contact information of any witnesses; call and wait for the police. Little did he know that the answer to his problem would come when he went to a presenation sponsored by the Ford Motor Company and delivered by Harold Smith in Chicago.

In the late 1950s to early 1960s, the Ford Motor Company thought it would be a great idea if its employees had driver's licenses; this way they could buy Fords. Out of the phonebook, they picked a fellow named Harold Smith to come and give driving classes to their people. As the story was relayed to me, one day when Harold was teaching his students, a couple of the Ford people came by and observed him. They were impressed with what they saw and heard.

They convinced Harold to shut down his driving school and come to work for them. Ford promoted Harold Smith's system as the answer to the problem of the large number of crashes. The deal was that if you bought enough vehicles in your fleet from Ford (cars, trucks, vans, etc.), Harold would come to your town and train your supervisor or your drivers in his 40-hour, in-vehicle, training course so that your drivers would learn to stay out of collisions.

In major cities, Ford offered a free one-hour seminar at which Harold gave an hour-long explanation of his system to anyone who attended.

It was an extremely effective system. It became known as the Smith System. The two fundamental concepts of that system are essential for collision-free driving. Every system that's based on collision-free driving follows these two fundamentals. It was such a valuable system that United Parcel Service (UPS) used it and then bought the rights to the Five Keys of the Smith System. Harold did a lot of training for UPS drivers. Mel Tracy, one of Harold's trainers, was one of the experts I had train a number of my staff.

Ford and Harold came to Chicago and Warren attended one of Harold's sessions. Warren told me his jaw dropped. He was in awe. "Holy cow! We could use this. We could implement this system and we could cut down the number of crashes that we're having. These accidents could almost become a thing of the past."

He was fortunate enough to get Harold to train his staff. Harold had dead time in between his road assignments for Ford. To spread these skills throughout the industry, Warren would schedule Harold to conduct training for driving school owners in the area Harold would be working.

Instead of three days of training on what to do when you were in an accident, Warren's instructors had five days of training in the Smith System. Accidents in Warren's fleet became virtually a thing of the past.

Years passed and Warren thought that the absence of accidents was no big deal. He assumed everybody had to be doing this by now. Harold had gone around the country and conducted numerous training sessions. Accidents no longer consumed Warren's time and the fear of having too many accidents had simply vanished.

THE MEN WITH TOP HATS AND FUR COATS

Warren sat at the long conference table in his office (at the corner of Foster and Elston Avenue in Chicago). He had a big, long, oval-shaped conference table next to a glass window that spanned the whole side of the room. It was a gorgeous place where we used to sit, contemplate, and have conferences or meetings. On this particular winter day, a long, black limo pulled up and parked right in front of his window. The driver opened the door and five men in fur coats and top hats stepped out of the vehicle. Warren thought, "Who are these guys?"

They came in to his office and sat down, and one said, "Mr. Rumsfield, we're your insurer. We're with Nationwide Insurance." They threw down the list of instructors that Warren had and they said, "We want to know where all the accidents are that you're hiding from us. We've got the driving records of your instructors and we're not getting any claims from you. We want to know where these accidents are because we don't want to get hit with a big lawsuit later on because you've gone out of business because of a bunch of accidents."

Warren said, "Whoa, I don't know about this." He called in Mr. Peterson, his manager at the time, and said, "Peterson, get the employment file for every one of the people on this list and on the outside of the file, in a nice, big, red marker, write the start date that these people began to work for us." Peterson left, got the information, came back, and dumped all the files on the desk.

All of the men from Nationwide began to go through each file. After they've reviewed every file, they looked at each other, looked at Mr. Rumsfield, and said, "Mr. Rumsfield, we're sorry to bother you. We don't need to talk any further. Have a nice day." They put on their coats and hats and walked out.

It turned out that every one of Warren's instructors had had their accidents prior to the time that they had begun working for Warren. Once they started working for Warren, they didn't have any more accidents. When the Nationwide executives realized that, they scooted out the door.

That's when Warren had an epiphany. That's when he realized, "Wow! This is unusual. We might be onto something special." He didn't realize just how special this was because when you're not having accidents, you don't think about them. You just start taking that benefit for granted. He didn't realize until that moment how powerful this training really was.

A similar thing happened to me. I mentioned earlier that when I went to the meeting in Toronto and I talked to the other driving school owners, they said, "Hey, we don't have collisions. Take the special training from this association and you don't have to worry about that." I thought that just couldn't be true. But I went back and took the training, and within a few weeks after I had taken the training, I said, "Wow, this something! We've never really done anything quite like this."

So I came back and implemented it at my school. I retrained all the instructors I had. Every new instructor who came in got a special retraining from them. Because of that, our business in Houston went for 11 years and over three million miles, teaching beginners without accidents—never once did our insurer have a claim from us. Do you think that is a system that is worth making available to every driver? How many lives could we save?

===

For FREE access to how drivers
can be trained to be collision-free drivers,
go to www.FREEdriverEdTexas.com.

===

CHAPTER THREE

WHAT THE ROAD LOOKS LIKE TODAY—DRIVER EDUCATION: FAILURE BY DESIGN

Most of you reading this have taken driver education. Whether your driver education experience was good, bad, or uninspiring, chances are you favor the concept that beginning drivers should be trained to become safe drivers and should be adequately tested before obtaining a license to drive.

Collision reduction is a noble cause, one that I have devoted most of my life to.

So why has driver education, after three generations, failed to produce safer drivers? Why are motor vehicle crashes still the number-one killer of teenagers? What are the problems with driver education and what are the solutions? Driver education is an example of failure by design.

The entire system of instructor preparation, curriculum development, regulation, and licensing, followed by testing, matches the typical public-school model. The emphasis is on theory, and teachers are certified or licensed based on their knowledge of theory; testing is predominantly on theory. Even the state road test requires only minimal skills. The courses are time-based, not mastery based. Credit is given for attendance and completing assignments in theory or engaging in specific activities. Testing has little relevance to real-world application.

No accountability, in terms of producing safer drivers, is built into the system.

As a group, driver education instructors have never learned what it takes to teach someone to become a collision-free driver because they themselves never had to learn how to become a collision-free driver. It's hard to teach what you don't know. Most of their training is done in the classroom.

Driver education instructors occasionally get in-vehicle training, but when they do, it's not much. Their training is predominantly in the classroom. If they do any instruction at all, they teach what they know: theory.

It wasn't always this way. Prior to the 1960s, almost all driver education was done by commercial driving schools and not in public schools.

The Federal Highway Safety Act of 1966 changed the landscape. The federal government threatened to withhold highway funds from any state that did not mandate driver education as a prerequisite for obtaining a driver license, establish rules and regulations for licensing driving schools and driving instructors, and create driver education courses for public schools.

Warren Rumsfield once told me that 48 of the 50 states complied without any hesitation whatsoever. They did not want to lose their highway funds. Driver education advocates promised a 50 percent reduction in crashes. *Highway Jungle*, written by Dr. Edward Tenney in 1962, documents advertisements that were put up by the AAA (American Automobile Association) and others claiming that driver education was going to reduce collisions or accidents by 50 percent. That promise was never met and remains unfulfilled.

You would think after three generations that we might have picked up on what we did wrong and plug in what works. Not so. Why is that the case? Why did that not happen with driver education?

Number one, the Federal Highway Safety Act of 1966 favored the implementation of driver education at public schools. Once that happened, any hope for accountability in producing safer drivers was gone. You've probably heard this: those who can, do; those who can't, teach. The corollary to that is: those who can't teach, teach physical education or driver education. Driving instructors are not the brightest of the bright.

After the law was enacted, driving instructors' status in the community became elevated. They were in a position where they were given a free car from a local automobile dealer. In order to drum up more business, the local insurance agent would have his or her picture taken with the instructor and run the picture in the local paper with a story of how they were supporting driver education with special insurance discounts for the kids. They had students who wanted to take their classes because they wanted a driver's license.

PHONY INSURANCE DISCOUNTS

The insurance discounts were phony. If everybody gets the discount, what kind of a discount is it? The discounts created the illusion that they were giving a benefit to the people who took driver education when the fact was, in many states, if you didn't take driver education, you couldn't get your license.

WHERE DID THE STANDARDS FOR DRIVER EDUCATION ORIGINATE?

In 1949, in Jackson Mills, West Virginia, the American Driver and Traffic Safety Education Association (ADTSEA) held a meeting. The meeting was attended, basically, by high-school driver ed teachers and the college professors who taught the courses that certified these teachers. They made a decision at that time to come out with a course that became the standard for the industry: 30 hours of classroom instruction and six hours behind the wheel. Look at their ratio. That's five hours of classroom for every one hour of practical instruction.

There was no evidence that this was scientifically proven to be effective, or that this was the ratio you needed to train somebody to drive. The reason it was done was because it fit into the traditional school model of one teacher to thirty students in a class. One-on-one, in-vehicle instruction is too expensive for schools to budget. The concern was what would fit into a public-school system, not what was needed to produce a safe driver.

Even though there have been some modifications by NHTSA and ADTSEA to those standards in the last decade or two, it's still the same ratio—that is, five hours of classroom for every one hour of in-car instruction, a seriously subpar standard.

WHY IS THAT?

They choose to operate with the notion that they have to get the students in, get them out, and make way for the next group. It's true in the public schools and it's especially true in the commercial schools, where the owner is looking at the fact he's got to put butts in the seats and then, as soon as their time is up, move them out of there, get them some hours in a car, and get them out because he's got to bring in more kids so he can collect money because he has bills to pay; he's got a payroll to meet. He can't wait until the kids master the skills to learn to drive safely; that's a luxury he can't afford. That's the mentality that exists in most driving school operations. And the public schools aren't much different. In fact, the public schools are even less flexible due to the rigid schedule they impose. Too many instructors are simply marking time and, in some cases, even cutting the course short in order to make ends meet.

An instructor or owner would say to a student, "Hey, you took an hour and man, you're great! You don't need the other four or five hours. I'm going to give you your certificate now. You're just a great driver." I've had parents tell me that. I had a school board member from the Texas Education Agency tell me that happened to one of his kids. The high-school football coach just brought him down after practice and said, "Hey, don't worry about that driver ed. Here's your certificate." The young man never took a class or any in-car instruction. The fact that this sort of thing has happened in the past is a good indicator that it is probably still going on now.

Even the very best schools, the ones that are above board and trying to do their very best, cannot produce a safer driver because the standards they adhere to require much more classroom time than in-vehicle training time. Driving is a psychomotor skill. A driver has to be able to look way up ahead, read the scene, anticipate the actions of others, create their space, and recreate their space as needed. This is in addition to their ability to manipulate the vehicle with ease. There's a lot going on that a new driver must juggle. In a mile, it's estimated that a driver has to make 119 decisions. You can't do that at the conscious level. You can only, consciously, handle half a dozen things, if that many, in a short period of time. Most of the decisions that are made in driving are made at the other than conscious level.

The training that most beginners get from public school or commercial driving school programs is in very basic manipulative skills. They may get some explanation of what they're supposed to be doing about reading and responding to the traffic scene. They may have even been introduced to the concept and told how to do it and maybe even practiced it a few times, but in the limited number of hours that instructors have to teach students, it's absolutely impossible for anyone to develop the neural networks that are required so that that prefrontal cortex establishes the patterns of judgment necessary for an automatic response to the variety of situations a driver is going to encounter.

A SYSTEM WITHOUT ACCOUNTABILITY

There's no accountability to produce safer drivers. Driver education is a once-and-done type of service. The students come in one time, purchase the course, and after purchasing it, either have a service they're satisfied with or not. If they're not satisfied with the result, well, that's too bad. Parents are not likely to send their child for additional training. The kids live (or die) with what they got. The kid could move the car and maybe that's okay, but that family is now on its own. In fact, that's why most states have a delayed or graduated licensing approach. The parent, or an adult with a license, is required or expected to provide supervised practice for the teen driver. The required practice varies from state to state. It could be from six months to one year or from 20 to 100 hours, usually with a few hours of night driving depending on the state minimum requirements. The fact is that any parent who is concerned about the safety of his son or daughter goes beyond those minimum standards. They practice until the teen achieves mastery of those skills. How many hours is that? That's whatever it takes. That's the real answer: whatever it takes.

It doesn't matter if they're in the parking lot 20 hours. They don't leave the parking lot until they've mastered certain skills. Mastery is the key, not the amount of time.

That's why public schools will never be a good fit for driver education that produces safer drivers. They are not designed to invest the large number of hours required for mastery. The school model is: 30 students to one teacher, fixed amount of time, little in-vehicle training. Is it any wonder that most of these new drivers know just enough to be dangerous?

The Insurance Institute for Highway Safety (IIHS) was a big supporter of driver education when it first started in 1959. The IIHS was founded by three major insurance associations that represented about 80 percent of the U.S. auto insurance market at that time. Their purpose was to support highway safety efforts by others.

When William Haddon Jr., MD became their president from 1969 until his death in 1985 he took a different approach. He looked at it from a more scientific point of view. He sought evidence to determine what would actually prevent crashes and reduce losses, injuries, and deaths. He was the first head of the Federal Highway Safety Agency (now the National Highway and Traffic Safety Administration, or NHTSA) formed when Lyndon B. Johnson was president and included as part of the Highway Safety Act of 1966. Every valid research of driver education at the time showed that driver education was not improving crash statistics or saving lives.

Consequently, the IIHS is now known for its safety rating of vehicles. It conducts and publishes crash test results, encourages standards for laws relating to drinking and driving and graduate licensing, and encourages parents to get involved in their teens' supervised practice. It engages in or publishes research related to these areas.

Why did the organization choose that course of action? I suspect that it is because results of the studies clearly demonstrated that driver education is not producing safer drivers. Counterintuitive as that seems, driver education has become part of the problem, not the solution.

The largest federally funded study ever done on driver education began in the early seventies with preliminary testing in the Kansas City area. Titled the Safe Performance Curriculum, it was commonly known as the DeKalb Study because it was conducted in DeKalb County, Georgia. The reason it was done there was because Georgia did not require driver education as a prerequisite for licensing. This allowed the study to have three groups:

1. A control group whose participants didn't have to take driver education to get their license;

2. A group that took the safe performance curriculum. The instructors and administrators of this program had everything they wanted: simulators, ranges, extended classrooms, all the in-vehicle instruction they wanted. This group picked its own instructors, and supposedly had the cream of the crop in driver education. It had leaders and college professors monitoring and guiding that course the whole way.

3. A third group that took an abbreviated course of driver education.

The study began with over 16,000 student participants. After tracking the driving records for a couple of years, then sifting through the data and conducting a follow-up to make sure that the data was as reasonably accurate as possible, the results were published.

The results? There was **no difference between the driving records of any of the groups.**

That's probably why learning to drive with a parent is the best kind of driver education. I'm not saying that every parent is more qualified than every instructor (although most of them certainly aren't going to be less qualified). What I am saying is that a parent who begins to teach a son or a daughter how to drive does not necessarily go at it with the same frame of reference that a driving school instructor or a teacher in a public school has. The "professional" instructor's frame of reference is: "I've got this much time and then we're out. Ready or not, we're supposed to be on the freeway today. If you can't get on the freeway, we'll ride around the parking lot. I'll still give you your certificate. Now you're on your own."

That's not what a parent is likely to do. A concerned parent is going to start to work with them and say, "Since we didn't get this done yet, we're going to have to practice it some more," or, "You're not getting it yet. I think this is going to take a little bit longer than I thought." The parent has the option of devoting the time needed to make sure his son or daughter becomes a safe driver and masters the skills necessary.

Parents are experienced drivers. They don't have to think about what they do when they drive. They just do it automatically, but that's not where a beginner is. A beginner needs to have some explanation, where to do it, what to do, why to do it, how to do it, and when to do it. That's really what we do for our clients and our parents. We give them the coaching materials so that they can become a competent instructor and work at their own pace. There's no fixed schedule that limits the students' ability to develop the skills. You finish when you truly master the skill, no matter how long it takes. When you master a particular skill, you move on to the next skill and so on. You take it a piece at a time, work at your own pace and under that frame of reference instead of trying to get a course done in a one, two, or three weeks, depending on which state you live in. The students will keep practicing until they're ready. If that takes six months, fine. If that takes nine months, fine. If that takes a year or a year and a half, that's fine too. The more time invested with an experienced driver guiding the beginner, the better. For access to our materials, go to **www. FREEdriverEdTexas.com** You can test drive these resources for yourself.

DRIVING TODAY IS RISKIER THAN EVER

Driving in today's environment is extremely risky, especially for beginners. Driving today is not like it was when you or I were teenagers. According to the Mayo Clinic, the **five major fears** that parents have about what could kill their teenage son or daughter are:

1. drugs

2. kidnappings

3. dangerous strangers

4. suicides

5. drive-by shootings

This is what's on the mind of most parents of teenagers and yet the leading cause of death among teenagers is motor vehicle crashes. Too many parents think, "My kid won't be in a crash."

The frightening thing about that statistic is that motor vehicle crashes have been the leading cause of death among teenagers for over three generations. It's just a shame that we have allowed that to occur and the reason we have is because we accept the status quo. "Well, that just happens to everybody. That's just how they learn." Many believe that after their teens go through driver education and get a license, the teen needs a big car that's already banged up a little. That way, when the kid wrecks the car, parents can keep their losses down.

In 1910 motor vehicle crashes accounted for the deaths of 3,503 teenagers aged 13 to 19, according to the NHTSA. If that were a flu bug, or if that were a shooting at a school, do you think it would have gotten our attention? You bet! You bet all the news stations would have jumped on it. But no, we just take it for granted. "So what? That's the way it is." It's just, "I'm sorry for their loss," and, "I hope it doesn't happen again." But there's no excuse for that.

Understand that young people aged 15 to 24 represent only 14 percent of the U.S. population. However, they account for 30 percent, or $19 billion worth, of the total cost of motor vehicle injuries among males and 28 percent, or $7 billion, of the total cost of motor vehicle injuries among females. The risk of motor vehicle crashes is higher among 16- to 19-year-olds than among any other age group. In fact, per miles driven, teen drivers aged 16 to 19 are three times more likely than drivers aged 20 and older to be in a fatal crash.

The U.S. Department of Transportation statistics indicate distracted driving contributes to as much as 20 percent of all fatal crashes and that cell phones are the primary source of driver distractions. Just imagine this: Sending or reading a text takes a driver's eyes off the road for 4.6 seconds. Wireless communication devices are so common that many drivers, both new and experienced, think they can safely text and drive or engage in phone calls and drive. It's not only the texter who suffers. It's the driver whom he texted.

We need to honestly address this problem. Having a wireless phone or a Bluetooth or a phone that comes through speakers does not solve the problem. Why? Because you drive with your mind and your eyes. That's right. You may not be looking down at your device, but when that call comes in, where does your mind go? It goes to the call instead of reading the scene. Unless you're extremely disciplined and can just ignore the call, ignore the radio, ignore everything else in there, you're likely to have a crash. That's why the only real solution is to shut off your communication devices when you get into a vehicle. That's it. Even if they belong to a passenger, you want to have them shut off when you've got beginners driving the car because they haven't developed the ability to tune them out. The added distraction makes them more likely to crash the car. This environment makes it much more hazardous for a teen nowadays than it did just one generation ago, let alone two.

Road rage is also something that is, unfortunately, a common experience but is a relatively new phenomenon. We had crazy drivers 30 or 40 years ago. There's nothing new about that, but there weren't as many of them, it seems, and they weren't as crazy. We always have had some show-offs. We'll probably never get rid of that, but the fact is that even women are becoming aggressive in their driving, not afraid to cut people off. Today in the United States, there are more cars on the road than ever before. The vehicles are smaller; their blind spots are greater (sometimes due to airbags and other safety features), making it more difficult for drivers to see if it is safe to change lanes.

Are vehicles today actually safer or more dangerous for teenagers? Well, it depends on your criteria for being safe. The design of many vehicles makes it difficult for a driver to check the blind spots. Certain technological advances claim to assist alerting the driver to objects in the blinds spots. The IIHS has led the way in encouraging and testing vehicle safety improvements. Improvements in vehicle safety and highway design are the leading contributors to saving lives. Overall, driver education (including traffic school and driver safety and improvement-type courses) has contributed very little to saving lives and reducing injuries.

In summary, with the current standards of driver education focusing on theoretical rather than practical skills and on just meeting minimum time standards instead of developing mastery of skills, we can expect to see driver education continuing to contribute to motor vehicle crashes by producing drivers who know just enough to be dangerous.

Keep in mind that there is hope. If we choose to look at this issue with fresh eyes, without the conditioning and prejudices of the past, if we clearly specify our goal (50 percent reduction in collisions) and choose a mastery-based approach, we could save thousands of lives and hundreds of thousands of injuries each year.

For access to free resources to produce safer drivers go to: www.FREEdriverEdTexas.com
Get one of our resources.
Let us help you save your teen's life.

THE SEVEN DEADLY MISTAKES PARENTS MAKE WHEN CHOOSING DRIVER EDUCATION FOR THEIR TEEN

During the eight years that I served as president of North American Professional Driver Education Association, I encountered several hundred driving instructors, driving school owners, and state and local administrators of driver education. Also, during that time and since, I've been involved in recommendations for legislation and regulations for the driving education business. I've designed and conducted conferences, workshops, and training sessions for driving school owners and operators, instructors, and instructor trainers. I've personally visited and interviewed thousands of parents and students and conducted on-site visits with driving school businesses from coast to coast.

What I have learned is that not all schools are the same.

This chapter identifies for you the seven deadly mistakes parents make when choosing a driver education course and what you can do to avoid those mistakes. This can help you make an informed decision that could help save your child's life.

Mistake #1: Trust the state to establish standards for safe drivers.

Mistake #2: Trust the driving school to produce a safe driver.

Mistake #3: Believe that caring is enough.

Mistake #4: Assume all schools and our courses are the same.

Mistake #5: Take the easy way out.

Mistake #6: Choose a program with little or no customer service or support.

Mistake #7: Fail to get a guarantee.

MISTAKE #1: TRUST THE STATE TO ESTABLISH STANDARDS FOR SAFE DRIVERS

We were brought up to trust police officers and firefighters. They were our neighbors. My mom used to tell me that if I got lost or was in trouble to look for a police officer. He could help me. I guess a lot of that trust was transferred to other branches of government and despite all the skepticism and disagreement folks have today about our government, I still believe that we live in the best country in the world.

Unfortunately, once a "system of laws and regulations" is in place in our society, it is not easy to change. It's like trying to turn the Queen Mary on a dime: it's not going to happen. The requirements for driver education as a prerequisite for obtaining a driver license seem to fall under one of those systems in which bureaucrats are entrenched in their ways and determined to keep their jobs.

What happens when our 15- or 16-year-old starts bugging us about getting a driver's license? We put him or her off, but we also start checking out what the process is for getting a license. We remember what it was like when we got our license, that scary trooper sitting there with his clipboard and gun. What a test of nerves that was! But we passed, got our license, and we walked tall, even if we did get a lousy picture on our license. Speaking of that, do they train people to take pictures that way: say, "Duh" and flash?

Well, things haven't changed that much, have they? In some ways, at least the ways that matter, the testing involved with getting a driver's license is still not that much of a challenge. You take a course, get a certificate, pass a driving test, and you're on your way. Despite all the evidence that traditional driver education has failed to produce safer drivers and despite the greater risk young drivers face as new drivers, the process has not changed much.

Why? Good question. There are probably a lot of factors. Parents and teens often don't think beyond what's most convenient or what the school they attend provides. Many simply assume that all schools and programs are the same. After all, they all meet state minimum standards. Who has the time to check out all the options with all the other things going on—work, ballgames, shopping, dance, church, doctor's appointments, band practice, and so on. Isn't that the job of the state to make sure that we have standards and that it's safe for our kids to go to school to learn what they need? Isn't it the state's obligation only to issue a driver license to qualified applicants?

That sounds good, and yes, there are some new restrictions in place to help young drivers gain more experience with fewer distractions, but they aren't solving the problem. There is no accountability built into the system. Understand that the state officials who get paid to establish these standards do not get paid for producing safer drivers. That's correct. There is no built-in accountability, no reward, no punishment. They get paid for meeting their job description and not for rocking the boat.

Do they get paid more for reducing collisions? No. Do they get paid less if there are more collisions? No. They get paid regardless of the outcome. Don't you think outcomes are important? What outcome are you looking for? You didn't invest the last 16 years of your life simply to lose your daughter or son in a stupid, preventable car crash.

So maybe trusting the state's minimum requirements for licensing is not such a good idea. Maybe you want to investigate a little, and do some poking around. Look for a course that has some built-in accountability. Find someone who's willing to guarantee his or her work. That's not too much to ask, is it? Who do you think is going to pay the price if your child is injured or killed, you or some bureaucrat?

I love the state of Texas and I believe the United States is the greatest country in the world. I wouldn't want to live anywhere else. However, all the evidence continues to show that our national and state standards for driver education have failed to meet their promise of safer drivers. We've had driver education standards since 1949 that emphasize classroom work over in-vehicle training even though motor vehicle crashes remain the number-one killer of teens. In short, you cannot trust the state standards.

MISTAKE #2: TRUST THE DRIVING SCHOOL TO PRODUCE A SAFE DRIVER

Who do you trust? There's a general notion that if you pay for a service, you are going to receive what you paid for. You trust that you shouldn't have to look over the instructor's shoulder and watch day after day, hour after hour, and minute after minute to see that the instructor is doing his or her job. That's why you're paying an instructor.

After all, these places are regulated by the state, aren't they? Yes, they are licensed and regulated. If the schools are in compliance, you at least have some minimal protection while your son or daughter is in the vehicle with the instructor. There are certain minimum standards they have to follow, but they simply are minimum standards. There is no requirement that a student be a safe driver when the student completes the course and gets a certificate of completion.

It might be worth your time to check out some schools that you are considering. Here are some questions you'll want to ask:

What do they offer? What types of courses do they offer, or do they only offer the one course?

What do they require? Do the schools require anything other than the state minimum? Does the student get credit for putting in time or does he or she have to completely master all the skills before getting a certificate? Be careful about this, because some will say, "Well, they have to pass the test." What are the tests? Mostly they're written tests that students have to pass and, of course, that's not the same as mastering skills.

Ask about their fees. Ask what they guarantee. Do they seem professional? Do they even answer the phone or do they use an answering machine only? If you're unable to speak with a knowledgeable person when you call, you may be disappointed or frustrated when you have to call to reschedule an appointment.

Ask them what curriculum they use. Is there anything unique about their curriculum? Who designed their curriculum? If the only answer is that it's a state-approved one, chances are this school only meets minimum requirements. Meeting minimum requirements is likely to result in a new driver who knows just enough to be dangerous.

Ask them what the collision rate of their graduates is. Now that's an important question. If they don't know the answer, that's a red flag right there; they are not tracking or paying attention to the collision rates of their students. Ask them how many times the driving school cars have been in collisions.

Also ask them if this course is a time-based course or mastery-based. Some of them may not even understand the difference. Ask them how long it takes the student to complete the in-vehicle training. If the student needs more practice, will they continue to do that for the fee that you originally paid them?

After calling three or four schools, you can begin to ask yourself whether or not your child is likely to become a safe driver if you choose one of these schools. Unfortunately, what you can often expect to get from a typical driving school are students who end up knowing just enough to be dangerous. They may know enough to manipulate a car. They may be able to start, stop, and turn. They may even be able to park, but they don't know how to critically read and respond to the traffic scene, how to create space, how to anticipate the actions of others, how to safely recreate their space when somebody steals it from them, or how to maintain emotional control.

As you go through this process, you will begin to realize that you cannot trust most driving schools to produce a safe driver. Instructors don't see that as their job. They see their job as putting in a minimum number of hours and then issuing a certificate so the student can get a license.

MISTAKE #3: BELIEVE THAT CARING IS ENOUGH

You may be willing to go the extra mile to give her opportunities such as ballet lessons, piano lessons, joining the scouts, or playing in your local soccer league. Frances got our boys into summer camps for computing and tennis lessons, swimming, gymnastics, dance, scouts, and marine biology. Anything they showed an interest in, she was willing to give them a shot. For her, no sacrifice was so great that she couldn't find a way. She'd help them do almost anything if they truly wanted it.

Being concerned is a great start. As a truly concerned parent, you've looked out for the welfare of your child for 15 or more years by now. You've comforted her when she was sick, and you've monitored her temperature when she had a fever, and you took her to the doctor to make sure that she got the professional assessment and the help that she needed. You probably read books to her, planned and celebrated her birthdays with parties, and did all the daily tasks that good parents do.

When you need outside assistance, you get it because you know that although caring is extremely important, it's not enough. With driver education, it's not enough that you care because you also need for your son or your daughter to care. Why? Because in order for your son or daughter to commit to developing the skills of collision-free driving, he or she must want those skills.

The reason that caring isn't enough even if you're willing to work with your son or your daughter for an extended period of time in your vehicle is that communicating with them about how to drive safely may feel awkward.

You know how to drive. You've been driving for years. You don't think about what to do when you're driving. You do it automatically. But to teach a beginner, you must communicate at the conscious level because that's where a beginner is. You need to explain what to do, when to do it, how to do it, why to do it, and where to do it, and those things are not going to come to you naturally because you're way beyond that stage and have been for decades.

The fact is that you don't know what it is that you don't know when it comes to teaching this on your own. That's why it's so critical that you have the resources that will enable you to draw on the wealth of experience that you have. You need to be able to ask the questions that will stimulate your child's prefrontal cortex, to allow your child to develop the judgment he or she needs to have. We're not talking just about muscle memory here. Of course, that is part of what you are teaching, but we're also talking about helping your child develop judgment and that takes practice and a lot of repetition.

Even if you have helped another son or daughter before and you are on your second, third, or fourth one, you must recognize that each one is different. The better the resources you have at your disposal, the better job you can do. That's why we provide resources at **www.FREEdriverEdTexas.com**. Get one of our resources to help you save someone else's life.

MISTAKE #4: ASSUME ALL SCHOOLS AND OUR COURSES ARE THE SAME

You would think that makes sense. Aren't all the schools licensed by the state? Doesn't the same regulatory agency also regulate and license the instructors who work in the schools? Yes. The schools and instructors are licensed and regulated, but only with minimum standards. There's little difference between the regulations for the public school and those for the private or commercial schools. There are a few schools that do their best to provide a good service.

Unfortunately, all many parents want is for the driver education to be over. They don't want to deal with driver education anymore than they have to because they've got other things to do. In fact, they'd prefer their student get a license to drive the car as soon as possible. Then they don't have to chauffeur him anymore. Better yet, let him chauffeur some of the other kids around and give the parents a little free time. Many parents are tired of being the chauffeur and want their kid driving. These parents don't believe that their child is going to be in a crash. Big mistake.

Here are a few suggestions to look for when choosing a driver education school or course:

1. Look for a course or school that guarantees that your teen will drive collision-free for at least one year. That first year is the riskiest period. The highest risk of being involved in a collision and getting injured or killed is in that first year. It would be nice to at least get a guarantee for that first year.

2. Find a course that is based on mastery of skills, one that is performance based not one that is time based.

3. Find a course that publishes the collision rates of its graduates, one that is based on actual motor vehicle records, not some survey with someone trying to get away with saying, "We had somebody call our people and they

didn't have any collisions." Most people have a selective memory when it comes to the collisions that they may have had. You need motor vehicle records to verify driving records.

4. Affiliation with state or national associations, unfortunately, offers no protection for you and your student. In the driver education and training industry, these groups are primarily self-serving organizations that promote a proliferation of laws requiring people to take their courses. They're out to serve themselves, not to serve the public. It's what some people call a racket: require people to take their course to get a license, thus creating a built-in market for course providers.

The truism that you get what you pay for certainly applies here. As the commercial used to say, "You can pay me now or pay me later." The problem is if you choose a driver education course based on its low price, the price you may pay later is often too high. You never imagine losing your child, but it can happen. The cheapest or easiest way out may cost you more than you can imagine. Do you believe that you get something for nothing? Of course not.

The reality is that individual, one-on-one instruction in the vehicle in real-world traffic comes with a price tag. There are real costs for the vehicle (insurance, fuel, and maintenance), the instructor, and the basic overhead to operate any business. Most driving schools (public and private) focus on keeping their costs as low as possible in order to stay in business and because they believe that the customer is only looking for the cheapest school and seeking only to get a driver license. Of course, there is some truth to that. Some customers are only looking for the cheapest schools and some are not concerned about their students becoming safe drivers.

You have to decide what's important to you and what you are willing to sacrifice to insure your child's safety.

MISTAKE #5: TAKE THE EASY WAY OUT

I understand that you have a very busy life. Most people do nowadays. You have things to do. You work. You run errands, you have more than one mouth to feed, you have bills to pay, doctor's and dentist's appointments to schedule and keep, a household to run, and often more than one kid to take somewhere. One has basketball practice. Another has volleyball, another swimming. Did anyone feed the dog? The list goes on and on. You know what it's like.

Now your son or daughter comes to you and says it's time for him or her to get a driver license. To get a license, you find out that driver education is required but the landscape has changed. It's not like it was when you were young. There are a lot of options that simply weren't available when you were learning to drive. In fact, chances are driver education might have been offered in your school or your child's school and you just automatically signed up for it because it was convenient to do so.

Since it's human nature to take the path of least resistance, you might go looking for the easy way out. That's why high schools used to offer driver education, not because it was an essential part of a well-rounded curriculum—which it isn't—and not because college admissions officers were scanning the student's transcripts for a driver education credit. It's because it was and still is an easy credit that made everybody happy.

Today in Texas, driving schools and at-home driver education courses approved by the DPS have become the primary delivery sources for driver education. Does that make your life any easier? Yes and no. Yes, because you have several options to choose from. No, because now you have to get involved. The more you participate in the process, the better the odds that your son or daughter becomes a safer driver. That is a consensus among every group that voices concern at the high number of teenage deaths and injuries due to motor vehicle crashes. Parental involvement is the key.

As with most things in life, we learn by experience, which means we learn by making mistakes. Unfortunately, with driver education, if you make one serious mistake, you may not get a chance to make a second mistake.

As a parent, you need a structure to follow and the right tools to make it safe enough for both you and your student. You are not going to have an extra brake to stop the vehicle. Your control comes via your communication skills.

That's why we provide the tools for you to know what to say, when to say it, why to say it, where to say it, and how to say it. Go to **www.FREEdriverEdTexas.com** for access to these tools.

You basically have two paths of involvement. You choose the type of course and the course provider, and you choose how much you plan to be involved. When you choose the type of course and the course provider, choose wisely. The information that we discussed in Mistakes #2, 4, 5, 6, and 7 should give you adequate guidelines for your choice.

MISTAKE #6: CHOOSE A PROGRAM WITH LITTLE OR NO CUSTOMER SERVICE OR SUPPORT

This is a big mistake a lot of people make. Most of the time when we think of customer support, we think of how a company responds to us when we have questions, or how the company helps us solve a problem we might be having with their product or service. Most of that customer service is handled over the phone. At least it used to be over the phone. Now, many times, customer service is done online via e-mail, texting, or chat rooms.

Whatever your preference, at least check out the customer service hours of operation and when it's available. You might be surprised at how important that can be when you're ready to take your son to the driver license office and wonder what you need to take with you.

Ask the school if your student will have the same instructor for class and in-vehicle training. Many schools randomly assign an instructor with a student. The student picks the time slot for the in-vehicle lesson and the school then assigns an instructor for that lesson. This impairs the student's progress because now, the process of establishing rapport, the process of discovering what the student's skill level is (identifying her strengths and weaknesses) starts over every time the student has a new instructor.

What do you think the odds are of producing a collision-free driver with that type of system? After each in-vehicle lesson, does the instructor take a few moments to update you on your teen's progress or is he or she too busy loading up the next group? When schools schedule instruction times back to back (a common practice), students and parents get less than they paid for.

One obvious need you have is how to do the in-vehicle supervised practice with your son or daughter. Depending on your goal, your situation, and the course you choose, you're going to need some help. Look for a course or school that provides you with access to the kind of tools you need to guide you through the process of coaching your son or daughter in the vehicle. Chances are you're a licensed driver with over 15 years of driving experience, but you don't think about how to drive at this point of your life. You just do it.

We've discussed this before. You need tools that provide you with a system for communicating with a beginner and sharing the wealth of knowledge and experience you have. We have such resources for you. Make sure that your driver education course or school provides these for you. You can always go to **www.FREEdriverEdTexas. com** and get one of our resources to help you.

MISTAKE #7: FAIL TO GET A GUARANTEE

Okay, you might be thinking, "Whoa there, pardner! What do you mean guarantee?" Very few businesses guarantee anything anymore. In fact, it has been my experience that only the very best companies even offer a guarantee.

What do you think a driver education school or course should guarantee? Remember, they're selling time not competence. Most of them only guarantee to take your money. It's up to you to do the rest. At least, you'd want them to guarantee that they'll show up for class when they're supposed to, that their instructor will be on time, that they won't cut the lesson short, that they won't be using their in-vehicle lesson to run personal errands, to go through McDonald's, or to sit around and talk about last week's football game at the local restaurant or drive-through when they are supposed to be out actually working with the student. Shop around until you get a guarantee that you're comfortable with and that indicates to you the school is holding itself accountable for its performance.

I believe it's the instructor's responsibility to ensure that the student becomes a collision-free driver. If your teen's instructor doesn't believe that, if he doesn't approach every lesson with that outlook, find another instructor or another school.

The purpose of a guarantee is to provide you with at least some degree of confidence in your choice of a driver education school or course. It should make you feel that not all the risk is on your end. We're talking about trust. Can you trust someone who's not willing to offer you a guarantee? Don't you feel a little knot in your chest or your stomach when you hand over your hard-earned dough and then wonder if this is really the best choice?

That's why a guarantee is important. It tells you that the person offering you that product or service is also taking a risk, making you a promise that if you do not get the agreed upon outcome, you get your money back. That's important. I hope you agree.

Isn't the outcome you want for your daughter or son collision-free driving, not just becoming another new driver who got a driver's license and knows just enough to be dangerous, or, in some cases, becoming a driver who is too afraid to drive in certain situations?

It's not unreasonable to expect your son or daughter to become a competent, confident, safe driver; that's what you're paying for isn't it?

Now you know the seven mistakes most parents make when choosing driver education courses. For our resources and tools to guide you through the process of coaching and supervising your new teen driver in the techniques of collision-free driving, go to **www.FREEdriverEdTexas.com** or call Driver Ed in a Box at 1-800-562-6405.

CHAPTER
FIVE

HOW DRIVER ED IN A BOX AND PATRICK BARRETT HAVE SOLUTIONS FOR YOU

As a parent, you can choose from one of three avenues we offer to help you ensure your new teen driver becomes a collision-free driver. And you have additional options with each one of these.

1. A complete training program: You can use Driver Ed in a Box to replace the driver education course or driving school you were considering (**www.FREEdriverEdTexas.com**).

2. A supplement: You can use all or part of Driver Ed in a Box to assist a new driver whose driver education only met minimum requirements, or if your son or daughter needs help in a specific area of instruction, or is simply afraid to drive (**www.FREEdriverEdTexas.com**).

3. Private Instruction: You can receive private, customized instruction through our concierge service from one of

our associates (**www.DriverEdinaBox.com/Concierge**), or you can receive an assessment and training from me personally. Please note: my schedule only permits me to accept a few clients a year (**www.DriverEdinaBox.com/VIP**).

ONCE-IN-A-LIFETIME OPPORTUNITY

As parents, you recognize that your son or daughter is not far from leaving the nest. Look how fast the first 15 or 16 years have passed. In two or three years, your young one will be living somewhere else. You now have a very limited window of opportunity to teach your son or daughter. This can be a wonderful, bonding experience that will be remembered for a lifetime. Why? Because we all remember where and how we learned to drive.

YOU BECOME A BETTER DRIVER YOURSELF

Two things are likely to occur when you teach someone to drive. First, you become a better driver because you heighten your awareness of how you drive. You realize how important it is to set a good example. You're not going to get away with saying, "Do as I say, not as I do." Example is a powerful teaching tool and knowing that provides leverage to keep you on the straight and narrow.

Second, anytime we teach, we tend to improve our own performance and analyze more thoroughly the distinctions we need to be aware of in order to teach.

We learn from what we know. The more we know, the more we can learn. And as the great basketball coach John Wooden used to say, "The most important things I've learned were the things I learned after I knew everything."

Driver Ed in a Box provides parents and their sons and daughters the structure, the tools, the checklists, the coaching tips, support, and the details to successfully teach them how to become collision-free drivers.

Learning styles vary from one individual to the next. Whether your student's preferential learning style is visual, auditory or kinesthetic (learning by physically doing something), Driver Ed in a Box has materials that address each style. No system is perfect in this regard, but we created videos, audios, and kinesthetic exercises in an effort to address all the major learning styles that people have. Of course, the in-vehicle training encompasses all three.

A COMPLETE TRAINING PROGRAM

Laws vary from state to state and your option for using Driver Ed in a Box as a replacement for driver education for minors may be limited by state law. You can check our website **www.DriverEdinaBox. com** to see what your state requires.

Driver education, where it is regulated, requires both classroom and in-car training. With Driver Ed in a Box, the classroom is in three parts:

1. Section 1, "Before You Drive" covers the basic rules of the road, traffic laws, driving procedures, what a student has to do to obtain a learner's permit.

2. Section 2, "Techniques for Collision-Free Driving," comprises the bulk of the material.

3. Section 3 is about "Consumer and Social Issues."

You can choose the above in three formats: 1) online only; 2) online plus the "Parent Tool Kit"; or 3) online + the Parent Tool Kit + the printed manuals.

After going through Section 1 and obtaining the permit (learner's license), you and your student move into Section 2, the "Techniques for Collision-Free Driving." For the beginner and the instructor, I believe this is the most valuable part of the training.

You review the 15 short videos from the perspective of the parent coaching the teen in the vehicle. You watch the parking-lot videos before you go in the parking lot, the neighborhood videos before you practice in the neighborhood, and so on. You watch the videos together. The videos give you, the parent and the student, a sense of what to do during the lesson. Watch the video as many times as you want to make sure you feel comfortable about what you're going to do during the in-vehicle session. The video sets the tone and also creates expectations as to what you are to do as the instructor and your son or daughter is to do as the student.

From the very beginning, your communication with each other is the key to a smooth lesson. You have specific terms to use and your "Parent Companion" provides you the list of terms (and definitions) and a checklist that helps you remember what to do from what you saw in the video.

This is critical. As parents, you are not going to have a dual-control brake in the car. The only control you'll have is your ability to communicate clearly, simply, easily, and quickly to your son or daughter. That has to be done in a fairly calm manner. There shouldn't be any rise in blood pressure in the process. You want to practice. Now where should you get this practice? Practice initially in a low-risk or no-risk area such as a parking lot.

There is no time limit in the parking lot. Be patient with yourself and your student. You are laying the foundation for communication, comfort, and eye movement. It's not going to be absolutely perfect. You're going to make a few goofs along the way, but that's all right. You'll catch yourself and adjust. You're the instructor, the one in charge, and you only let that vehicle go where you want it to go.

How do you accomplish that? With your questions and commands. There are actually specific language patterns you use to control the vehicle and to control what the student does. There are different language patterns that you use to let your student take over control; the amount of talking is still the same, but you use it in a different fashion. You use different phrases, and you use specific questions to help guide the process along. This enables the student to eventually perform without your assistance. You learn how to do that through our audio series.

Should you rush through the process? That depends on your goal. I'm never in favor of rushing through any area of instruction. Repetition (correct repetition over time) is necessary to build the neural pathways needed for habitual behavior. Also, different seasons of the year expose the student to different driving conditions. That's why it's so important to practice anywhere from six months to a year. It's not enough that your student has mastered those manipulative skills, that she knows to turn her head at an intersection, or that she does the one-two-three count and understands how to pick the path of least resistance. As you are aware, different times of day and different times of year bring about different circumstances. Because of that, you want your students to have a variety of experiences (day and night) so that by the time they start driving on their own, there is very little that they haven't seen or haven't had to deal with. You want their fundamental processes so ingrained that even if something out of the ordinary comes up, they are going to automatically know what to do, and respond correctly. When that occurs, that's when you know you have done your job well.

One additional note about the commentary: There are 86 terms or phrases. Basically, there are three categories of commentary terms. There are the words that are *nice to use,* and you like to use because they help to create awareness, they help you know what the student sees, and they create clarity on how the student is interpreting the scene. These are also phrases that help you communicate to the student what you would like to see. Then there are the phrases that you *should use,* the next most important level. You want to use these phrases, but you're going to use them only for a limited period of time or until the student has integrated them into her performance. And then there are the phrases that you *must use.* These terms you must use all the time. By the time you get to the end, depending on your point of view, there are only five to eight terms that you want to be using absolutely all the time. That's it, just a handful that you constantly need to be able to use because they are critical if you wish to imbed collision-free driving skills.

Section 3 includes all the things that a driver needs to navigate through social and consumer issues. They are designed to meet the requirements of the state and prepare your teen for "nontraining" issues related to driving.

The topics in Section 3 do affect a person's driving. There are six class hours of the effects of drugs and alcohol use. Then there is a bonus video on drug and alcohol. It's the true story of an Olympic athlete, a diver who was the heir apparent to Greg Louganis, the great diver for the United States. Richard Kimble was in Florida, training for the Olympics. He went out one night, had too much to drink, and was driving drunk when he killed two teenagers and crippled at least two others. It's a gripping and compelling story. Additional topics include distracted driving, impaired driving, peer pressure, road rage and emotions. In addition, there are chapters on how to buy and sell a vehicle, how to insure a vehicle, how to maintain a vehicle, new technology in vehicles (a video on how the anti-lock braking system, ABS, works) and the impact driving has on the environment.

WHY WE PROVIDE YOU WITH TWO INSTRUCTOR MIRRORS

Imagine getting in your car to start a lesson with your son or daughter. Your student assesses for you the six conditions that affect driving and makes the necessary adjustments before starting the vehicle. Then you whip out your sleep mask or a scarf and blindfold yourself for today's lesson. Crazy, right?

But that's what happens when someone tries to teach without two instructor mirrors.

One of those mirrors is a rearview mirror for you. It allows you to see what is going on behind you, so you won't ask your son or daughter to make a lane change when there is a vehicle about to fly by. Do that and your student will think, "I need to make a lane change because Dad told me to." Then all of a sudden, boom! You get side swiped. Your student says, "I knew it was there, Dad, but you told me to go." We actually teach you how to prevent that from happening.

So that's why you get a rearview mirror. It comes with a little suction cup. It doesn't block your student's view, but it allows you to see behind you, and without that you are coaching blind.

The other mirror that we provide you with is an eye check mirror. It's a round, flat mirror, also with a suction cup, and goes in the top right corner of the front windshield. That mirror enables you, as the parent, to coach your student on eye and head movement without staring at her and making her more nervous than she already is. It is critical that you coach your student to learn how to move her eyes every couple seconds. You do this by asking questions and glancing in the eye check mirror to see if she has moved her eyes or not. You can also check to see if she moved her head enough to expand her peripheral vision at intersections.

Once the student realizes all that she has to watch for, it drastically alters her attitude. "This is not as easy as I thought it was. This is going to require a little more effort on my part. I'm going to have to pay a little more attention. I'm going to have to be on the ball a little bit more here," she will think. This awareness helps modify her behavior, which modifies her attitude, which influences her behavior (a cybernetic loop).

YOUR DRIVING JOURNAL

Another great tool we provide for you is the driving journal. This is a journal that allows you and the student to write down your "aha" moments. These include significant moments when they have that breakthrough, what they've learned from it, and what could make their driving better. You could write about lessons that weren't perfect, and those that will be good to talk about later on. Years later you might have a conversation such as, "Oh, remember that. I can't believe you told me to go when that truck was barreling down on me. At least one of us was paying attention." Short notes can lead to long stories. It's fun to laugh at our mistakes years later, and you can show the grandchildren what their mom or dad went through. Take a few pictures and videos to make your stories more memorable.

You'll also receive a **student driver sign** that you can put on your vehicle. It's not a permanent type of sign, so you don't have to use it all the time, but some people like to have it on while they are moving along in the neighborhood and the parking lot to let other drivers know that they are teaching a student driver. Some people like to have it in light traffic. Of course, when you complete everything, you can receive a certificate of completion, which in some states is accepted as proof of completing a state-approved driver education course.

ADVANTAGE SAFETY CLUB

Another bonus is that you get automatic access to our Advantage Safety Club. Now, what is the purpose of that? We produce an in-box magazine (*Ready to Roll*), an e-mail newsletter that we send out with reminders and coaching tips. You also can get our monthly newsletter (*On the Road Again*), with stories, updates, and special offers plus additional coaching tips. A number of driving instructors who receive this have told me how much they like it because it reminds them of things to do. These reminders help you stay sharp and the stories, games, and puzzles are fun.

MONEY BACK GUARANTEE

You get our unique money-back guarantee. We guarantee that your son or daughter will drive his or her first year collision-free or we refund the course fee. Now, there are some caveats with this. I do not want to sanction illicit behavior. I don't think it's appropriate to reward someone who has been driving while intoxicated, or driving under the influence of drugs. So if that occurs, the guarantee is void.

If the new driver is out joyriding between midnight and three in the morning when prohibited from driving because of a restriction on the license, we are not going to reward that sort of behavior. If students do something that is completely reckless, if they are racing the car, or if they get a ticket for reckless driving, for putting other people at risk with aggressive driving, or if they are engaged in a wireless communication just prior to or during the collision, the guarantee is void.

If you follow the program, and we have agreed that you have followed the program when we issue you a certificate of completion, during that first year, if your teen is in a collision, we give you your money back. There are claim forms that a claimant has to complete, such as providing a police report, and a letter from the insurance company confirming a claim was paid. We review everything and talk with the student and the parent. By interviewing the parent and student about what happened, I can discover if there is something in our course that we need to do a better job of communicating. Most of those who have had collisions have one thing in common: They stopped doing the commentary or did very little commentary. They admitted that they used a few terms, or the parents thought it was silly, or they abandoned that part of the training. They thought they were smarter or the commentary was too much work.

I talked to one student who said she was at an intersection with a stop sign, where she had been before, but she just forgot to stop. She ran the stop sign and caused a collision. Of course she was at fault. I started questioning her and wondered how that could have happened. I asked about her training experience and specifically about what happened during the commentary.

She replied, "We didn't do that too much; we did a little bit and got tired of it, so we stopped doing it." Then it dawned on me.

That's probably why she had the collision. I didn't say that to her, but I had a pretty good idea that's exactly what happened because if you are reading the traffic scene and you have done this over and over and over again, doing that commentary every time you approach an intersection, that commentary is going to stick with you. Do it a few thousand times out loud and it becomes a habit for you. If, as the parent, you have asked the questions we recommend thousands of times when you train your student, eventually your student will think of those questions herself.

"PARENT COMPANION"

Your "Parent Companion" has everything you need to keep on track and make sure you don't leave anything out. It's a great tool that allows you to log your time, and check what has been mastered and what is not yet perfect. It references all the commentary terms and includes diagrams you can use when you're teaching in the vehicle, and in-vehicle tests to help you and your student measure your progress.

FREE DRIVER EDUCATION

If you want to test out our resources and content, you can go to **www.FreeDriverEducationTexas.com**. Our mission is to help you and your family become collision-free drivers, so if you need to try it before you buy it, that's okay with us. You have options with our resources, through our subscription site, where you could just pay for what you need on a monthly basis. You could order just the videos, or just the mirrors; you could pick and choose what you are going to have and use it for as long as you need it. You're in charge.

The fact is, almost every state in the United States now requires parents to do some type of supervised practice. Choose one of our resources to help you guide your son or daughter through the process of becoming a collision-free driver. Too much is at stake for you to watch from the sidelines, so get in the game.

PRIVATE INSTRUCTION

This is an option. I accept a few private clients every year. My fee starts at $75,000. With the time I have left on this planet, I have to be very selective about how and with whom I work. However, I have a number of associates I can recommend whose fee is considerably less (**www.DriverEdinaBox.com/Concierge**). Should you feel the need for private, customized, one-on-one instruction you can go to our website at **www.DriverEdinaBox.com/VIP**.

Sometimes, as parents, we forget how important we are to our children and what memories we are creating. The following is my story (that is included in our *Driving Journal,* one of our resources for you) of a memory of my dad.

"A DAY AT THE SHOP"

We got up early in our house. Well, when I was eight years old I thought it was early. But on Saturday, I liked to get up early; that was the day Dad would take me and my brother Jay to the shop.

My dad had a sheet metal business that he grew into a heating and air conditioning business. I really didn't know much about that sort of thing when I was eight. All I knew was that on Saturday I got to spend the day with my Dad. That's what made Saturday so special for me and that's what made getting up at 6 a.m. an easy thing to do. Truth was, Friday night, when I went to bed, I was already thinking about Saturday with Dad.

Jay's my older brother, just a year older, but still he's my older brother and the oldest boy so he gets the window seat. We're about to head off to the shop in the old red truck—it was a Ford, circa 1953, if I rightly recall. It had a little oval on the center of the steering wheel and a starter pedal on the floor to the right of the accelerator that Dad had to push to crank up the engine.

After a couple of tries, Dad gets it started, and away we go. We drive with the windows down and we always go the same route: Elm Street to State Street. As we go past St. Peter and Paul Church—we called it the cathedral—we're at the top of a hill and we can see the Mississippi River. That big, old river is there every day. What a sight. We descend down State Street on a hill that curves to the right. There's a stop sign at the end of the hill right next to Mr. Sager's drug store.

Dad goes to the next block where the fire station is on the right. We all wave to the fellows (the firemen) sitting outside the firehouse on a couple of chairs. Then Dad makes a U-turn and pulls the truck up to the shop.

Jay and I hop out and stand at the front door of the shop waiting for Dad to unlock the double doors so we can start our work day.

The shop has a brick and concrete front that rises about two to three feet from the ground and the rest of the shop front is all glass windows. On the left-side window are hand-painted letters that read, "James J. Barrett, Sheet Metal." The shop, at 327 State Street in Alton, Illinois, was started in 1896 by my great-grandfather. Because State Street slopes downhill toward the river, one end of the shop is higher than the other.

Our first job of the day is to lower the awning. The giant green awning was held up against the building and tied off at both ends like a flag on a flagpole. Jay and I each untie one end and then lower the awning. The awning keeps the sun off all that glass in the afternoon and helps keep the front office cool. It also provides shade for folks who stop by to chat with Dad before they begin their hike up the State Street hill.

Jay and I move sheets of metal that were delivered on Friday from the floor into the bins. These sheets of metal are about eight feet long and three feet wide. Jay and I are used to this job. We work pretty well as a team because if we're not careful, those sheets of metal can slice up a hand or a forearm in the blink of an eye. It was not uncommon to come home with cuts on the palms of our hands. I never got used to that.

Dad inspects our work and we get to sweep the floor. Then we get to make S-slips and drives, small pieces of sheet metal that we bend and fold. They are used to hold the duct work together.

First, we cut left-over pieces of large sheet metal into smaller pieces (about three inches or so). And if you're not careful with this machine, you can slice off a finger. It'd be like a knife going through soft butter. So we respect this machine; no horseplay during this job.

After we cut the pieces to the right size, we go over to the machines that bend or fold the sheet metal.

The machine we use to make the drives is run with a small motor. We snip the front corners of the sheet metal at a 45-degree angle with a pair of tinner's snips (a tool for cutting sheet metal) and feed the metal through the machine, which folds metal so it comes out the other end of the machine flattened and ready to use.

The machine we use for the S-slips is sort of a minibrake; a brake is a large piece of equipment used for bending large sheets of metal. We slide in the metal, clamp it down, fold it, release, fold it again, release, repeat the process once more, and then press it all together. When you view it from the end, it looks like a squashed "S"—pretty cool.

Throughout the morning Dad spends more time with us than he does in the office. Mostly, he's making sure that we are doing the job correctly so we won't get hurt. But he also leaves us alone long enough for us to feel that we don't need someone standing over us to do our job. I get the feeling he really trusts us.

Around one o'clock or so, Dad comes out of the office. Once again, he inspects our work. Then he asks if anyone's hungry.

Next stop: the Green Lantern. Dad, Jay, and I sit at the lunch counter of this small diner and we each get a hamburger, fries, and a soda. Wow! This is great. Jay and I are the only kids in the place; we're eating with the men.

While we eat, we listen to Dad telling his buddies he's got his top crew with him today. A lot of the men look at my brother Jay and say something to Dad about how they broke the mold with him.

After a satisfying lunch, the kind where your belly feels full but not too full and you can still taste that root beer in your mouth, Dad takes us back to the shop.

We have a gutter to paint for a job that is being done on Monday, so Jay gets most of the paint on the gutter; it goes on the inside, not the outside, but some of the paint drips to the newspapers on the floor and, naturally, some of it gets on us. Then we clean the paint brushes, hang them from a nail in turpentine so they won't get stiff, and wash up so we can head home for the day.

On the way home, Dad goes down a few side streets, points out customers' homes and tells us which job he did at each one of them.

Dad pulls into the driveway and parks the truck between the back of the house and the big oak tree and says, "Boys, you did a great job today. Thanks a lot. Did you have fun?"

Jay and I nod and grin from ear to ear.

It has been a great day, a day with our Dad at the shop.

A NOTE FROM THE AUTHOR

The sheet metal business my great-grandfather started in 1896 has gone from "James J. Barrett Sheet Metal" to "Barrett Heating & Cooling." When my brothers and sister took over the shop, they needed a bigger place, so they bought a building around the corner and fixed it up. Dad gave the shop site and building to the public library. Technically, he sold it, but for the price he got, I'd say he gave it away. As I write this, the shop is celebrating its 117th year in existence—not bad for a business started by a poor but industrious Irish immigrant who came to America because of a potato famine.

The shop has moved from its original location at 327 State Street to 500 Belle Street, just around the corner (see the picture of the current location; the shop still has a big green awning!).

Six of my brothers and sisters work at the shop today and most of my nieces and nephews in the area have worked at the shop at one time or another, whether it was part-time after school, during summer, while they were going to college, or while they were between jobs. Two of my nephews have been full-time employees for several years and it looks as though the shop will continue at least through one more generation.

Pictures: top left - the shop at 327 State Street; top right - the shop at 327 State Street with the awning down.; bottom left - author's father, John J. Barrett, Sr. (WWII photo); bottom right - the shop today at 500 Belle, Alton, Illinois

Take this opportunity and build great memories with your son or daughter.

CHAPTER
SIX

TRUE STORIES FROM THE DRIVER ED IN A BOX FAMILY

n this chapter our clients do the talking. Because of the limited space, we can only share a handful of stories from the tens of thousands we have received. One of the things that impress me most is our clients' awareness, especially the students' awareness, of what is necessary for them to become a safe driver. It shows a great deal of maturity.

Who are Driver Ed in a Box clients? They, like you, are parents and students. They take learning to drive seriously. They are:

professional athletes, actors, actresses, state and local law
enforcement officers, FBI agents, schoolteachers, professional driver
education teachers, accountants, engineers, military personnel,
home makers, entrepreneurs, small-business owners, secretaries,
administrative assistants, homeschoolers, sales professionals, nurses,
and others in the health professions, legislators, writers, film makers,
scouts and scout leaders, singers, songwriters, band members,
robotics engineers, athletes—including volleyball, basketball,
football, soccer, swimming—cheer leaders, and the list goes on.

And they represent all regions of the country from Alaska to Alabama,
Texas to Minnesota, California to Connecticut, New Mexico to
New Jersey, Colorado to Tennessee, and Oregon to Florida.
Public and private schools—including a school for the deaf—have
invested in Driver Ed in a Box.

But the common thread among almost all our clients is that they care enough to realize that driving is a dangerous task, and they want to learn to drive well, not just so they can move the vehicle and get a license, but so they can become collision-free drivers.

I was at a homeschool show when a young lady and her mother came up to me. I started to ask some questions, and the mother promptly said, "You don't need to tell us about the course. We were here last year and we looked at everything that was available and my daughter said this is the one she has to have." I went to get her paperwork and her box to get her started and the young teen paid for it herself. She pulled out these fives and these ones. Maybe a twenty was in there. Her mom said she had calculated what it would cost to purchase her Driver Ed in a Box program and had taken all of her babysitting money for the year because this was the program she wanted. It didn't matter to her that it was a little more expensive than the others. She knew this was the one that would suit her well.

I think there is a lesson there for all of us. That is, if we make a commitment and are willing to work for it, even if we have to delay the reward, the reward means more to us. The feeling of earning something is much better than the feeling of being given something. There's a sense of pride, dignity, and self-worth that you get from earning something that is missing when you are given something.

I know in my own family the prizes that my sons, John, Michael, and Warren earned from selling scout fair tickets when they were young were the things that they cherished more than Christmas or birthday gifts because they had earned them. I suggest parents should help their sons or daughters do something to earn their driver's license. I know it's not always practical to work outside the home, but there is always something they can do to earn it, to feel that pride of ownership, that they earned their way to this privilege. Learning this lesson is important, since we want drivers to become responsible drivers.

It was a heartwarming experience for me to have that young lady pay me directly with her babysitting money and walk away with a smile, knowing that not only did she get what she wanted but she had earned it.

Another thing that consistently happens at shows and conferences is that folks will come up to me and thank me for the course. "Oh, we used this program and it was great. It will be several years till our next one, but we'll be back. We think everybody should be trained this way. All new drivers should have this kind of training. We wish you could do more to promote the program."

That's one reason I'm writing this book.

It's as if I'm sitting on the cure for cancer and only a few people are looking for the cure. They'd rather keep the cancer because that's what they're used to or they don't believe effective training or coaching can make a difference; more likely, it's because most driver education courses are a waste of time and resources.

Here's a letter from Katie Clemens, a student from Boerne, Texas.

> *First of all, all I want to say is that normally my mom and I do not get along. I mean, normally we cannot talk together about anything. Because inevitably, we strongly disagree, and both of us end up angry and frustrated. BUT believe it or not, Driver Education in a Box actually brought us closer together. For the first time since I can remember, my mom and I could work together, and it was amazing. We had a common, calm, productive, learning experience. My mom admitted that she was reminded of traffic laws and regulations that she had not encountered as a driver, yet if the situation were to come up, she would know the right thing to do.*
>
> *We started out the program a bit hesitant. But before long, we could not wait to find the time to work together. We listened to the audios and watched the videos together. Some we watched several times over. My mom, who has been driving for years, explained some of the terminology and gave real situational examples of how these concepts would be put into practice, once we started driving together. My first time driving was amazing. Oh sure, I was a bit hesitant, but because of all the coursework before my mom would let me drive, I felt completely prepared, and ready.*

Mom and I would practice, by calling out my actions before I would make a turn, that way she would help me to realize the potential hazards I might encounter as I drove. (Which actually felt a bit silly because I was in an enormous EMPTY parking lot.) Slowly we progressed to the back roads around our town. Luckily, Boerne, Texas, has a lot of empty roads, where we were able to practice. Later, we would drive on open highways, then around Boerne itself. As we drove, my mom would intentionally create difficult scenarios for me that I may not see in day-to-day driving, and this was amazingly helpful. She would have me on dirt roads where the car does not stop quickly, and on hilly paved narrow roads where I would have to interpret signs on the road side regarding who has the right of way.

We drove in hot sunny weather, where glare shines up from the road, creating a sort of illusion, then really hard rainstorms, where the roads became dangerous and slippery, and where washes are truly life threatening. Like I said earlier, it was really nice driving around with my mom. We would drive for miles and miles and miles, no radio on, just the two of us chatting. Mom would quiz me from the book, remind me of laws and regulations, and even now that the program is over, she still quizzes me, saying things like, "What speed limit is required by law in this pedestrian zone?" The more we drove, the more competent and relaxed I felt. The course-work solidified the essential knowledge that is required to be a collision free, law-abiding, safe driver. But I have to say, it was the hours of time behind the wheel that this program allows. It was the flexibility that really prepared me to drive

in the unpredictable environment, where driving takes place.
Thank you for creating such a program.
Sincerely,
Katie Clemens, student
Boerne, Texas

Well Katie, thank you for the beautiful letter that you wrote.

Katie's letter is instructional in a number of ways, one of which is the notion that she didn't think the program was going to work. The main reason for that was her inability to communicate easily with her mom. That is something that both a parent and a student should honestly assess. Oftentimes you might think, "I can't do this, because we just don't get along that well. We just end up fighting a lot. I don't have the patience with her." There probably are times when that is absolutely true. But that doesn't mean that you can't do this. If you are willing to make the adjustment to be a little patient, to be a little more understanding, to take a breath, step away, and ask yourself what is the best way to do this, you sharpen your skills as an instructor, take pressure off the student and make the lesson a lot more fun. Remember, you both have a common goal: that your son or daughter becomes a collision-free driver. Focus on that outcome.

I think Katie and her mom are a great example of what you can do if you are willing to take the time and allow things to blossom.

Now here is another comment:

My parents chose to do the Driver Ed in a Box as opposed to a traditional driving school. At first I was shocked, nay, horrified! How was I supposed to get to know the ways of the road without a professional guiding me through each and every painstaking step? That, however, was not an issue. The

genius of Driver Ed in a Box is they developed a program that makes you feel like you have a professional teaching you. The innumerable training videos and the well-thought-out curriculum, made it feel as if some man with gray hair in a far away land was teaching me. My parents were rather more like tutors or advisors guiding me through the process—it was such a visionary experience. Every lesson was, without a doubt, completely necessary to my experiences on the road, and I have yet to regret any second of it. With only my parents on the seat next to me during my first time on the road, I was filled with terror. What should happen if I were to freeze up in the middle of an intersection? Or clip the curb in the rain, and go careening around the highway destroying everything in the path of the giant metal death trap, which is this automobile? After long moments sitting in white-knuckled silence, however, my classroom lessons began to filter back to me. I began to regain my composure. The calm that I felt could only be a result of the hours of preparation and intensive study that brought me to that point. I realized I had been equipped with all the necessary skills by my classroom experience, and my parents (as always) were there for my safety. I set out, and everything went exactly according to plan. Nary a clipped curb, or destroyed guard rail in sight. At every intersection, I did exactly as the book instructed me, it was amazing.
Student D. J. M.
Alvin, Texas

DJ thank you very much for the letter. Again, this is instructive in several ways. First of all, I find it interesting that he starts out his letter by saying his parents chose to do the Driver Ed in a Box. It's interesting, because sometimes parents don't want to be parents; they just want to be friends; they want to be buddies. They don't always want to make the decisions that are appropriate for them to make. And, like in the example before with Katie's mom, that parent made a choice as to what she was going to do, and in DJ's situation, they made that choice because they thought this was in the best interest of their child, their young adult. They chose to help their child become a collision-free driver.

Now I don't know if they already knew how ineffective driver education courses are in public schools and almost all commercial schools, but that didn't matter. What they knew is what they were willing to do.

DJ felt as if I were instructing him. How does he know I have gray hair? Great compliment, DJ. Thank you. Students I personally trained have told me that when they drive, they can still hear my voice in their head.

I feel successful when the student gets a sense of my voice being with them, guiding them through this material, as well as coaching their parents through what to do, when to do it, how to do it, why to do it, and where to do it. It makes the parents themselves feel as if they were professionals. The parents gain additional credibility because the student realizes that this isn't something Mom or Dad made up.

Our next letter comes from student Jordan Lorch from Cypress, Texas:

Doing Driver Ed in a box has been wonderful. I can teach myself the information in my own time, and I don't have to modify my schedule to get to a classroom for hours on end to listen to this information. With the videos, I can play and pause them at my own pace, and I can ask my parents questions whenever I want, compared to waiting for the appropriate time to raise my hand in a classroom. I can go get my learner's permit whenever I felt the time was right and I don't have to wait till I pass the test and have the instructor's permission to take it. With Driver Ed in a Box, I pick my time of day for the drive times. I don't have to wake up at 7 a.m., or go right after school when I'm concerned about other things. Learning at my own pace has been great. Without the classroom distractions of other students, I can focus on my lesson, and learn every detail that my instructor has said. By knowing the person who is teaching me, I feel much more relaxed and comfortable in the driver's seat. I feel relaxed asking questions of my parents, and driving with them. While driving, I don't have another student in the back seat distracting me, as I learn to drive, but as I get better, my parents will let my siblings drive with me as I learn and begin to feel comfortable driving, even when everyone else around me is loud and distracting. I feel that I am becoming a great driver because of my dad's knowledge of driving. Driver Ed in a Box has been an easy, relaxing experience and I feel confident with my driving skills.

Wow! Thanks a lot, Jordan. Again, there are some parts of your letter that are instructive. We design a program that **allows a student to move at his or her own pace.** Much of this will allow students to progress without a parent standing over their shoulder all the time, checking to see if they are doing something, and the program allows students to gather the information and take the quizzes at a comfortable pace.

As Jordan points out, you can stop the videos and go back over something. Also, anytime that he had a question, he didn't have to hesitate or wait until the classroom teacher thought it was an okay time to ask a question. Many times, when students in a class setting ask a question, the instructor doesn't respond or doesn't recognize the students, or might even make fun of them with a remark such as, "Well, that's a stupid question! Who knows the answer to that? I can't believe you weren't paying attention." The student's confusion might very well be a reflection of how poorly the instructor explained the concept. But a lot of instructors are defensive, assuming the student's at fault for not paying attention.

You must understand what occurs in a classroom setting. Most of you can relate to this, if you've attended meetings, classes, seminars, and so on: you have been listening to the speaker, but your mind suddenly takes off on a tangent, and you begin thinking about what the speaker has just said. In the meantime, the speaker continues and now you've missed whatever they have been saying, or at least you haven't caught all of it because you have a question that needs to be answered. Your mind begins a transderivational search. It goes through the reticular activating system, the file cabinet in your brain that allows you to hunt for things, sort through them, and piece them together. That's a very normal response. In a traditional classroom setting, a lot gets lost.

Because Jordan was able to do the course at home at his own pace, when he could schedule it, not when he felt pressured to get something else done, and not at a time of day when he wasn't sharp, he could focus on what he needed to do. As any of us know, when we can focus clearly without distractions, we can get a lot more done. That's a real benefit to using this particular style of teaching.

KNOWING THE PERSON WHO'S TEACHING YOU

Jordan raises another issue that I think is very instructive when he says, "by knowing the person who is teaching me, I feel much more comfortable and relaxed in the driver seat." Young people are often uncomfortable with a stranger next to them. This is especially true when they are in a situation in which they have to perform, and their performance is being judged. At this stage, the student's skill level may be weak. Consequently, the student is afraid he's not going to do well. He fears being embarrassed. He may make a mistake and have a near miss, a hard stop, or a crash. He doesn't want to have that happen.

All this is magnified when there is somebody in the back seat. Unfortunately, in a lot of schools, there isn't just one person in the back seat; there may be two or three people back there, horsing around, doing who knows what, and the instructor's attention is now divided between the people in the back, and the person in the front, the traffic scene, and the clock. This is a very poor system. Having one or more students in the back and one in the front increases liability because it is likely to create distractions that put extra pressure on the new driver. Jordan talks about how his parents would allow him to drive with his siblings in the back, when one of his parents was in the front. He learned how to drive safely no matter what distractions were going on. The ability to screen out distractions from inside the vehicle can be learned. In fact, it is a great training session to have, not at the beginning obviously, but later on, as an advanced lesson.

A lot of driving schools—I mentioned this earlier—tend to switch instructors around with a student. They are just filling slots. They have the "get them in and get them out" mentality; that's just how it works. Now, when a student gets in the vehicle with a different instructor, the whole process of developing rapport has to start over again. The whole process of identifying where this student's strengths and weaknesses are has to begin again. Even if the instructor has some sort of checklist, the notes don't tell the whole story. The instructor probably does not know that student's particular idiosyncrasies. Instructors tend to get in the car with students and simply ride around with them. They have their own route, their own way of teaching. You would think that professional instructors would adapt their teaching styles to the students. Far from it. In almost all cases, the students have to adapt to the teacher because teachers have their own set ways. They get into patterns of behavior, certain things they teach, certain things they do, and if the students don't adjust to them, that's the students' problem, not the teacher's. Kids either adapt to the instructor or they lose out.

Notice there is an element of self-doubt. Both Katie and DJ thought, "Gee I don't know if I can do this." That's not uncommon. In fact, even parents occasionally experience their own self-doubt about whether or not they should teach their son or daughter. Self-doubt is okay. You can overcome self-doubt with preparation and action.

YOU'RE ALREADY TEACHING WHETHER YOU WANT TO OR NOT

As a parent, you are already teaching your student how to drive. From the moment your son or daughter watched you behind the wheel and thought, "I could be doing this one day," they've been paying attention to what you do. They know how you turn the wheel. They know what you do as you approach a stop sign. They know what you do as you approach a stale green light or a solid yellow light at an intersection. They know how closely you follow somebody. They know how hard you brake. They know if you have an abrupt lane change. They know all those things. They may not be completely conscious of these events, but they have witnessed your driving thousands of times when you transport them from one place to another. Don't think that hasn't made an impression; it has.

It's not a question of whether or not you are going to use parent-taught driver education, or whether or not you are going to teach your son or daughter to drive. The fact is you already are, and have been, teaching them how to drive. The questions are: What have you been teaching them and what are you going to teach them, going forward?

With the materials that we created in Driver Ed in a Box, you can actually teach at the same level, or even better, than most "professional" driving instructors.

Why? Because parents come from a frame of reference that is completely different from that of the driving instructor. Parents are there to make sure their son or daughter practices and learns specific skills of collision-free driving, not just to manipulate the vehicle, but to read and respond to the traffic scene in such a way, and until such time, that they can do it by habit and become a reasonably safe driver on their own. Most "professional" instructors work through a minimum number of hours as required by the state for their students to pass a very minimally challenging state road test and get a certificate. That is the difference here. If you think you can do a better job, you are like many of our clients. And if you are willing to invest a bit of time to follow the program, listen to the audios, and watch the videos, you should be very pleased with the results.

Raising a new teen driver whose life is going to be at greatest risk during the first year of driving is a challenge. And the benefits go beyond safety. One of the most frequent comments we get from the son or daughter is, "I was so grateful my dad spent that time with me. That was our time together. He took time out of his schedule, and that was our time together." As a parent, you may not realize how important it is to your son or daughter. It matters, it is important, and it makes them feel important to you.

These are only a few examples of how folks like you use Driver Ed in a Box and why it is unique.

If you have any additional questions, or feel you need any resources to help your son or daughter become a collision-free driver, you can go to **www.FREEdriverEdTexas.com**, get one of our resources, and let us help you save someone's life. It just might be the life of your child.

COLLISION-FREE AMERICA: HOW YOU CAN JOIN THE CAUSE

IS A COLLISION-FREE AMERICA POSSIBLE?

R ealistically, we're not going to get rid of every car crash in America. But can we do better? Yes. Can we cut the collision rate by 50 percent? Yes, if we have the will to do so. Can we accomplish that through effective driver training and not simply through the redesign of vehicles and roads and effective law enforcement? Yes.

The improvements that have occurred so far in the reduction of the number of deaths are largely due to traffic law enforcement, redesign of the highways, and redesign of vehicles. Recently, the number of deaths among teens has begun to climb, no doubt due in part to the use of wireless communication devices (texting) while driving. Very little improvement has occurred because of driver education. I'm including the driver education that beginners get, and also the ongoing driver education that others get, through their workplace—generally through some type of classroom course referred to as driving safety—or defensive driving, or driver improvement courses, which include what are commonly referred to as ticket dismissal courses, or traffic schools. In fact, traffic schools probably are the best example of the real blood money that's in the driver education business, an industry that exists primarily because of legislation spearheaded by course providers. Are the driver education industry and its supporters likely to be part of the solution? Not likely.

AN INDUSTRY THAT EXISTS BECAUSE OF LEGISLATION

I don't know what you do for a living, but chances are you actually have to do something that creates value for your customer. You create or deliver a product or a service that meets some need that an individual or a company has. Your clients are not required by law to purchase your product or service.

But the driver education industry exists primarily (in some cases, solely) because of the laws that require people to take these courses. Take away the legal requirements for these courses and you'd see a different industry.

These laws exist because the vendors, the providers of these courses, get state legislators to enact laws that require people to take their courses. Parents and other citizens don't object either due to apathy, a blind trust in government officials, or a transient interest (they only have to deal with this issue when their teenager wants a license to drive). Often, it takes years of persistence to enact laws and the driver education lobbyists keep coming back until they get what their clients want. It takes time, money, and effort to influence legislation. Individual parents don't see this as their role and are at the mercy of what the legislators pass into law.

If you look at the states that have no driver education requirement, none whatsoever, you'll find very, very few driving schools, and little driver education being carried out in those states' school systems. Why? Because, most people, if they are not required to take driver education, won't take a driver education course. If driver education had fulfilled its promise of reducing collisions by 50 percent, no one would question its value. But it has never happened.

ONLINE COURSES ARE A SCAM

Today, the big push in driver education is online courses, as if that's going to make someone a better driver! In fact, it's a big scam that the industry has cooked up to generate revenue. And it's a shame, because all the time, resources, and money that go into creating these courses and requiring people to take them for the profit of the few who operate them have very little effect on producing safer drivers. If we put the same effort toward courses that created value for the client, that actually did some real training where people improved their driving, we could make a big difference in this country in terms of reducing the collision rate.

Ticket dismissal courses and traffic schools offer very little benefit. At best, they may produce the Hawthorne effect. The Hawthorne effect originated as an industrial experiment in Cicero, Illinois, at the Western Electric Company. The test was to see if worker productivity improved with a change in environment. The lights were turned up and then turned down. A slight improvement was seen in worker productivity for a very limited time. And that's about it. That's about all you will get out of some of these courses. This means that there may be a little improvement for a very short period of time, and then, none whatsoever, hardly worthy of the time, effort, and resources spent on the course (unless you're the course provider or the regulator).

I'm not against driving schools making a profit, folks. We live in a country where profit is a desirable motive. And it is necessary for us to work in a capitalist system. The problem isn't the profit motive; the problem is there is no accountability for producing safer drivers. If we can get driver education out of the public schools and, as individual consumers, expect and demand instructors and course providers of driver education to be accountable for making the student a collision-free driver, we could cut our collision rate in half.

How do we solve the problem and what can you do to help save lives?

YOUR OPPORTUNITY TO MAKE A DIFFERENCE

You have an opportunity to make a difference, to make our country a safer place to drive. How?

First of all, accept the fact that if you drive a vehicle, you're either part of the problem or part of the solution. There's no middle ground. At the very minimum, resolve to do your best each and every time you drive. You could leave more space between your vehicle and the vehicle you're following. That alone will make a difference.

If you wish to do more than set a good example, here are seven ways that you can partner with us to serve the Cause for a Collision-Free America.

1. If you are a parent or grandparent (step-parent or step-grandparent) get one of our resources and supervise your

teen's driver education and/or driving practice. Collision-free driving skills are acquired through structured practice with spaced repetition. These skills are not intuitive and do not come naturally. Our resources include a booklet, "How to Tell … Will Your Teenager Crash the Car? … Try These Tests," which contains 39 sure-fire tests any parents can use to check out the safety level of their new driver (now available from Amazon.com, Kindle).

2. Volunteer to speak to parents and teens about collision-free driving through Driver Ed in a Box resources and our associates—**www.DriverEdinaBox.com/ourmission**.

3. Volunteer to coach new drivers using our tools to assist them in becoming collision-free drivers—**www.DriverEdinaBox.com/ourmission**.

4. Become an instructor on a part-time or full-time basis. You can become certified through one of our training programs At **www.DriverEdinaBox.com/ourmission**.

5. Operate one of our Certified Safety Centers for Collision-Free Driving. My good friend and mentor, Warren Rumsfield, used to say to me "The people who will help us train safer drivers are not yet in the industry." Imagine how many lives we could save if we could repopulate this industry with folks who were concerned about producing safer drivers, not just helping someone get a driver license—**www.DriverEdinaBox.com/ourmission**.

6. If you are a driver education teacher or a driving instructor, you can upgrade your skills and begin to assist your students in a mastery-based approach to produce collision-free

drivers. I believe there are a lot of honest, conscientious instructors out there who would do a complete job if given the opportunity. If you are tired of only meeting minimum standards and turning your students loose before they are ready to drive on their own, contact us at **www. DriverEdinaBox.com/ourmission**.

7. If you are a driving school owner or a driver education administrator, you can use Driver Ed in a Box resources to improve your school's chances of producing collision-free drivers. I believe there are a lot of driver school owners and driver education administrators who truly want to produce safer drivers but feel limited by minimum state guidelines. If you are interested in helping your instructors and your customers become collision-free drivers, contact us at **www.DriverEdinaBox.com/ourmission**.

And remember, every time you drive or you practice driving, practice as if your life depends on it—because it does.

If you're an individual who desires to make a difference, someone who wants to help others reduce their chances of being involved in a driver-error collision, you need to contact me at **www.DriverEdinaBox.com/ourmission**. We need you. America needs you.

CHUCK'S STORY: A SENSE OF CONTRIBUTION

Around 2003, Chuck Dunbar, a friend I had worked with in other businesses and met playing basketball at the YMCA, started to help with our marketing. Initially, he was a contractor—a vendor—who did some marketing for us and then eventually became a full-time employee who handled all our marketing for several years until he was diagnosed with renal cancer in 2009. Chuck had been in a number of sales positions. He had been the head of sales for a number of companies and was very successful. He told me that none of his sales jobs—while they were all fine—had ever made him feel that he was doing as much good as this particular job did. And then he told me, "Pat, you don't realize that most people go through life with jobs that are not that significant, jobs that don't really impact people, and don't make them feel great. They don't get that wonderful sense of contribution and accomplishment. They don't experience people coming up to them at events and say things like, 'Oh, thanks so much for the program that you made. We've used it. It's worked well for us, and our kids have still gone without collisions for years. We're so grateful that you made this program.'"

Chuck told me that working with us made a difference in his life. He felt that he actually was doing something that was making a difference. It wasn't about selling a product or service for the sake of making a transaction; he felt a sense of purpose and fulfillment with Driver Ed in a Box.

I want to thank you for taking the time that you've invested in reviewing and reading this material. I know that if you've read this, chances are you're with us already, you're someone who wants to be part of the solution, not part of the problem. So please, feel free to contact us by going to **www.DriverEdinaBox.com/ourmission** and tell us how you would like to contribute.

Folks, we can actually reduce collisions by over 50 percent in this country. I know this because I've done it. I've done it with every group that I've ever worked with, and I've been able to work with beginners to help them achieve that. Now, obviously, I can't person-ally teach everybody. It's just not going to happen. But what I can do, and what I have done is create the materials and the processes for people to teach others, to help them become collision-free drivers. If you're willing to participate in that and follow those guidelines, we can actually reduce collisions in this country by over 50 percent. I have no doubt about that.

The question is whether you are willing to get involved. Are you willing to take a step and do something about it? This is especially important for parents because the fact is that you're training your children anyway. But, again, it's not whether or not you're training them; it's what you're training them. Those of you who are no longer parents, whose kids have grown and are gone, may be in a position to help improve this horrible situation. The rate of collisions, crashes, deaths, and injuries to our young people is extremely high, yet preventable. If you want to do something about this, you're welcome to do so. You simply need to go to our site at **www.DriverEdinaBox. com/OurMission** and send us a note about what you're willing to do or how you'd like to participate. What you do matters.

Take action now. Go to **www.DriverEdinaBox.com/ ourmission** and tell us your area of interest. Let's make America a safer America.

Study of Texas DPS Teen Driver Records

Driver Ed in a Box Produces Teen Drivers Over Nine Times Safer Than Other Training Methods.

Sixteen-year-old licensed drivers in Texas have a collision rate of 11.4 percent (2001 data).

Sixteen-year-old drivers trained with Driver Ed in a Box have a collision rate of only 1.74 percent (2005 data).

The collision rate is calculated by the number of collisions reported to the Texas DSP, as reflected on individual driver records, divided by the number of licensed drivers in that category, multiplied by 100 to convert to a percentage.

SIXTEEN-YEAR-OLD DRIVERS

The 2001 Texas DPS's "Motor Vehicle Accident Statistics" report shows 141,357 licensed 16-year-old drivers had 16,113 reported collisions for a collision rate of 11.4 percent for that year.

In April 2005 a random sample of 1,009 Driver Ed in a Box 16-year-old graduates' driving records were pulled directly from the Texas DPS records. The Driver Ed in Box 16-year-old graduates had only 14 collisions for a collision rate of 1.4 percent in 2004.

In 2006 a follow-up study of another 1,018 randomly selected driving records of Driver Ed in a Box showed 16-year-old graduates had only 21 collisions for a collision rate of 2.1 percent in 2005.

SEVENTEEN-YEAR-OLD DRIVERS

The Texas DPS statistics report referenced above shows 181,014 licensed drivers aged 17 had 19,517 collisions for a collision rate of 10.8 percent in 2001.

In 2005, a random sample of 553 records of 17-year-old Driver Ed in a Box graduates show only five collisions, for a collision rate of 1 percent for that year. A 2006 follow-up of 1,018 Driver Ed in a Box 17-year-old graduates' driving records, randomly selected, shows only one collision for a collision rate of 0.1 percent for that year.

COMBINED STUDY

Driver Ed in a Box Graduates

	# Collisions	# Driver Records	Collision Rate
Age 16	35	2,097	1.7%
Age 17	6	1,571	0.4%
Total	41	3,560	1.2%

Texas DPS Report

	# Collisions	# Driver Records	Collision Rate
Age 16	16,113	141,357	11.45
Age 17	19,527	181,014	10.8%
Total	35,630	323,371	11.0%

SUMMARY OF 16-YEAR-OLD DRIVERS
COMPARATIVE COLLISION RATE:

- Driver Ed in a Box graduates (2005 data): 1.74 percent.

- Combined graduates of all methods of driver education in Texas (2001 data): 11.4 percent.

For further information, go to
www.DriverEdinaBox.com/ourmission
or contact patrickbarrett@driveredinabox.com.

How can you use this book?

MOTIVATE

EDUCATE

THANK

INSPIRE

PROMOTE

CONNECT

Why have a custom version of *Warning*?

- Build personal bonds with customers, prospects, employees, donors, and key constituencies
- Develop a long-lasting reminder of your event, milestone, or celebration
- Provide a keepsake that inspires change in behavior and change in lives
- Deliver the ultimate "thank you" gift that remains on coffee tables and bookshelves
- Generate the "wow" factor

Books are thoughtful gifts that provide a genuine sentiment that other promotional items cannot express. They promote employee discussions and interaction, reinforce an event's meaning or location, and they make a lasting impression. Use your book to say "Thank You" and show people that you care.

Warning is available in bulk quantities and in customized versions at special discounts for corporate, institutional, and educational purposes. To learn more please contact our Special Sales team at:

1.866.775.1696 • sales@advantageww.com • www.AdvantageSpecialSales.com

Printed in the USA
CPSIA information can be obtained
at www.ICGtesting.com
JSHW012056140824
68134JS00035B/3467